RAYS OF GROWTH

GROWTH MINDFULNESS AND WELLBEING

ODAI ABDOU

This book is dedicated to my family, my father, and mother who supported me during the whole journey while I was still a child tell I started to work on my goals in life, and to the people who have supported me during my career, and have never lost faith on me, this book is a work of years and years of leering and searching it is dedicated to the people round the world who seek knowledge and wisdom.

Contents

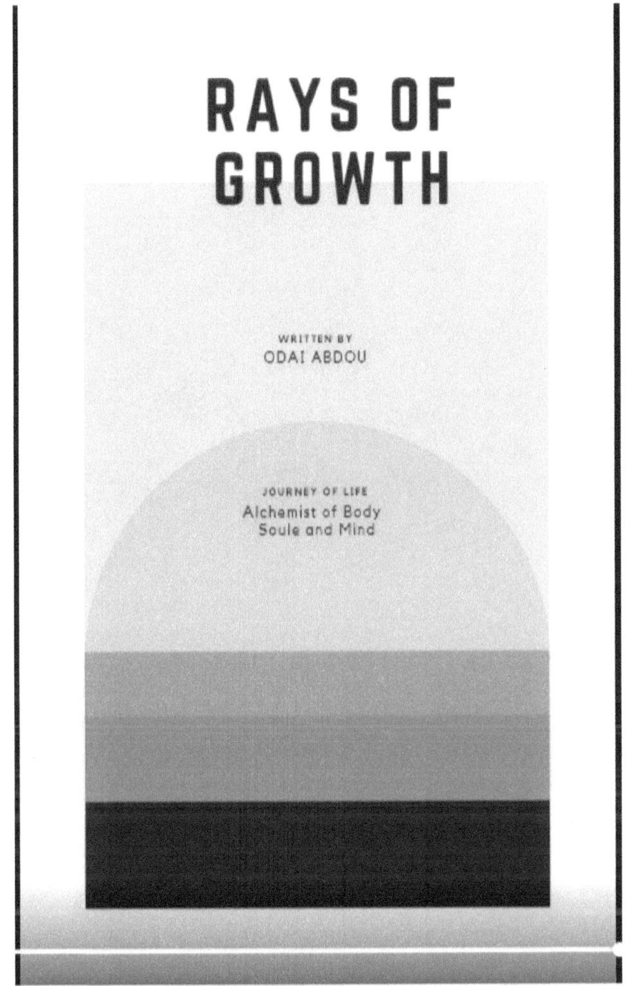

Enter Caption

CONTENTS

ONE
JOURNEY

•ᏢᏢ•

Journey

Day in time

(**suffering is not bad , suffering and losses are a pass and way of creating personal heroism , people who suffer the most gained the most**)

adayeh lived in a place where there was an economic struggle that was not healthy.

You had to deal with a lot of problems when going through your daily routine, the sound of cars rushing to work, people coming and going to work, the sound of birds waking up- in the mooring then the clock is 8 nearly 9 AM in the mooring you need to get out of bed and start your day jumping to your reality. He recalls believing that he was going to finish my degree and go on to a new chapter of his life while I was in my last year of college in Economics at University. Everything around him was a mess, the road, the people, my thought was that everything has to be better than that and I need to run away from this and find a better place where he doesn't have to face any problem and no disruption to me, a place where he can just wake up and find peace and happiness he was thinking was so annoyed by my reality that he wanted to search for such thoughts while on my way to school

He would go back to my routing where he set his self-up and wash my head, he take his breakfast meal for a local traditional food and he try to catch my class at 8 a.m. so he can feel like he is really doing something and not wasting my time and I am on my way to do something, he is on his way to change my situation from bad to good from down to up, after he finish my class and return home and his energy starts to slow down a lot and he feel like he don't have to do anything anymore he just need some sleep and to close my eyes from this reality, and suddenly i forget about all the problems and plans that were inside my head and he go back to the rest zone let me call it where he just need to feel relax and safe on my bed and dreaming about nothing maybe just fading away and finish my day by going to bed maybe before going to sleeping go to entertain myself with some kind of move or a television show or a games on my mobile that is it but it's after all temporary and he is going to just close my eyes and start feeling tired , all of this routing makes feel like you are being lived or you are attached to a game or some kind of prison inside and you have to deal with anyhow .

he had one problem that he used to care what other had to say about me and I would watch Cleary and pay attention to every world they might say about him if its good it makes feel proud and happy and if it's bad or criticism its made think that how they are so wrong eventually it's just that its human nature to search for perfections and color life and Rinbo and all of that

staff , Udayah brother was used to live in India since he was doing his Ph.D. there in Economics at Mysore university India , he has been living there for almost a two years , and own used contact him from time to time and without knowing that his brother is living in a different country and culture . own mother was a housekeeper and his dad was an electric engineer who used to works in ships and travels for m0nths and seals and sometimes for more than one year, his smaller brother was still doing his high school he was a very young boy talented and so keen into tech and video games his English was so good , anywvay Udayeh after his final year completed he had to live Syria especially that he had graduated from school and need work or Elsa to continue his master study , since the economy in Syria was doing very bad , and the war was still in its begging most of the young people used to do the same in order to escape and search for a better future , the civil war in Syria has done so much effects on the people and there was almost nothing pushes you to stay inside the country , So Udayeh find a way that his brother would finds him a master course to do in India in Mysore city and that what happen , joseph his big brother has admitted him at Mysore University for a master degree in Economics , Udayeh start working on his visa and passport as soon as he done with his documents he booked a flight to Bangalore which a state near to Mysore city only after 3 days of getting the visa to India , hoping that he could find a better place to start his new journey with the world and so he did , he packed his bags and staff and went to India , as soon as Udayeh landed in Bangalore airport in

India he could feel that

A new journey has begun and that he is going to search for a new way for his life , he went inside the arrival hall and check his passport at the immigration he was so nervous and tires but also he was happy and filled with joy and excitement that his journey has just started his destiny has brought to a new line in his life , he could finally feel the freedom , since in his country the oppression and inequality was dominant , the ruler family and the government was not working for the benefit of the people in Syria , instead they were working for the benefit of protecting its place , Syria one of the richest country on earth , richness in culture and civilization not only oil and green lands , Udayeh felt that when he landed in India he could finally feel the real freedom of abasement and injustice that he suffered in his country and his people as well .

As soon as he arrived he collected his bags and went to outside street where he saw the city and people of India for the first time and he went to the bus stop that take you to Mysore where he was hiding to, his brother was supposed to pick him up from the airport so he wait it . not soon enough his brother came and meet him they both took the bus Mysore and took off to Mysore it took them around 4 hours they finally arrived to the Mysore which is the cleanest city in India , it was a very beautiful and clean city , with a lot of green parts ,tall trees and long roads , it was not so crowed but so much of a calm and easy to get used to .

They both reached home and sort it out the place where they supposed to sleep and Udayeh felt it's a new place far. Away from home and so long ago Udayeh start preparing for his life .

He started he master degree as a normal student he looked to finish his course and move to a new way of life but out of nothing , he first went to his class it was full of Indian student and he was the only Syria their he felt little bet lonely and stranger in few moments a couple of international student just entered the class , his new classmates one was from tablets china his name was Tenzin and one from Vietnam his name was shu one girl from Kenya she was very smart and neat her name was Halima , , those friend where his new friends he start chatting with tensing he looked very integument and funny smart easy to go with they sat next to each other and felt and began to exchange talks and questions , both Udayeh and Tenzin become friends , Udayeh started to know more about other culture and how that he was living in his country Syria closed away from other culture and civilization suddenly he started to love what he was discovering and told about the other world he know that there is always and new roads another place to start the life And t3est the way of living he almost felt as if he is leering again about the world and how big it is and not what people are talking about in his community in Syria .

So Udayeh finished his class and went home , , arrived home In Mysore city talk shower , had food with his brother and took a nap , at the evening he walk up study a little bit and started the chatting his brother about what he is finding in India and how beautiful Mysore is , he knew that his country was totally different in Mysore , in Mysore they were using English language and kannada language as a way to talk and speak to each other he felt that he has to start leering and train on speaking English abet more so that he could be more adaptive and active .

((Always look up to yourself as the main character of your own story , make your self-matter when you don't think you are))

Mysore was a very calm city a green city you call it's a place where you truly can find the peace and happiness that you can urge in your life YOU CAN TASTE THE power of love and happiness in the eyes of the people in Mysore , you can feel the energy of the nature blessing around you , you will since the living and wellbeing raising and dancing around you in Mysore from the small tiny insects to the brides , and cows and cats , every living creature is just running and living in his own circle of life .

Udayeh was experience the nature again in way that he did more discover before in his life the sky was blue the air was clean and cold, the street where clean and organized , the people where moving and running in all directions .

Udayeh meet his firmed was named jadeh form Mysore his friend started telling him how beautiful is Mysore city and how he people of Mysore live a simple life he told him that in Mysore people to like to stress them self they take everything in simple way and avoid violent and harm actions , their best idea of living is to choose the smile way , the act of being kind to each other , and with the people of Mysore used to live like that , Udayeh was impressed by what his friend saying he thought to his self that why not why not being kind to each other , why no we always reach to our positive side rather than just hitting on each other , why note we create small smile on our face and be winner and be little kind to each other cause you know after all know one is taking to his pocket a thing for the other life after life .

If you go all over the country and even Asia and asked about the name Mysore , everyone will go and tell it is one of the best place to visit in India, not mention that this green amazing place has been awarded the cleanest city in the country five time , the people of Mysore understand English very well , don't worry if you don't know Hindi it is a great way to bond with the people .

Udayeh remember one day that a saying in the old thought of an old civilization the once life begin to trouble always remember that there a new door of good is opening for you and for that you should always find what is the that shifting inside you what is that one thing that changing inside your mind , seeing all people wondering and smiling around , catching your breath after running , smiling at a stranger makes you feel that there is a something that I holding our life towards the best for the future .

Udayeh continued his way home and felt that life could really mean something and that they're always thing in life that we feel we are con3ected to and we need to just express our self just about the right way . living in a different a place hearing a different language and a culture this could always mean that you are challenging yourself your habits and your own endearment that you used to live in and raised in , once you had the time to live and experience a new adventure your will feel the joy and blood running in your vessels once your know that your put your first steps towards it.

The way you shape your reality comes when you decide that you have a new hope a new plan to build your own track and road for the future it is always the experience that live within us so once Udayeh start living every day and enjoying the moment he felt that he is not missing anything he is always catching up with the university and just joggling around the event and getting in only what is matter which is having fun doing what you love and what you are built to do on earth , something you need to remember that it is the small thing that build up for the big things

Udayeh went on the next day on a small trip with his friend joseph to chamandi hill, in Mysore for you if you don't know Chaminde hill .. it is a very beautiful hill in Mysore city almost mean the near the side of it .there are many famous gurus that has visited Chamindi hill in Mysore such as the great Indian sadhguru who has visited chamnidi hill ansd talk about in his book human engeeinring and has said how he used to climb chandihll all the 1000 steps all the way to reach to top after that he sit on the rock which from there you can see all of the Mysore city up from there , it such a magical place said Sadghuru , there is a say in Mysore that goes like this , if you are happy then go to chamindi hill , if you are sad go to chamindi hill , if you are bored go to chamindi hill, if you are depressed then go to chamindi hell , if your happy then go to chamindi hill , it is just like as if it's a very spirit and special place that you can go and release you energy there and spend some time doing so .

Udayeh released then that he was in a very special place chaminid hill for all Missourian and every person from outside Mysore , the road to chamindi hill where a very well organized and built , on the way to chamindi hill you can see cars and buses moving to the top , once you reach up in the top of the hill you will start feeling something special that you are in the top of the sky you can see small plane flying next to you , the city view for math stop is so amazing so the advice is that you go there and you sit on the two looking down to the city view from up and you do something meditating and something spiritual calling were you can you jump into peace state and clear you mind , the idea of that chamindi hill represent the part of your mind that is alone and peaceful and creative , and when you reach that state of mind you can relay feel the you self that you are really alive , just feeling the air and sun light in all of that the eyes close but not your imagination. Udayeh felt that there is something special about this place , something that were hiding and soaked inside every stone and plan around this hill when he first came here

And when you finish your meditation and all what you need after is just keep silence and enjoy the nature , the sky above where the clouds are just moving away , the birds flying into the space , how can be such a magical place around us and we cannot notice that , if we always look carefully we will always find some peace and magic .

Udayeh was one day with his friend aliah who told him once that there is a prominent figure is coming to Mysore city soon and that he wants to join that , so he asked Udayeh if he want to accompany him to this event so Udayeh said yes why note , what and who is this figure asked Udayeh , well he is a very spiritual and a mystic guru that know all around India , he has been known for his wisdom and imagination that speeded all over the world and almost everyone is fascinated about him , Udayeh got excited once he heard that and he wanted to go and meet him by attending his sessions in Mysuru as everyone likes to call it .

So the next day Udayeh went to his university for his master course he know that his trip in india was not by mastic or luck , he know that he has to start build his life and find Purpose in his life , once you start living the joy the real joy of life which is the feeling of the present and thinking clearly about your existence by truly looking around and wondering about the elements of the nature , Udayeh back to his house and rest at knight , start looking at the starts and he found that every time he really found he has been not enjoying life and missing many thing around that really make your eyes glomming and your head blowing away by the way they were put together and how they are functioning , take for example the sun how big is and how small it is from a distance

Alchemist Energy

How can you always close your eyes and just forget about the world and your problem in the works , and start diving into your mind and you will realize that averting is living inside your mind and not the opposite .

The next week Udayeh went and attended the speak of sadhguru in Mysore and he so fascinate about the wisdom and the idea that he bring to the ears , sadhguru has his own unit way of talking whenever someone asks him he used to answer clearly and calmly he first start to speak with a minute of silence and then he put his head down and say well it's a great answer he takes his time and find the best words to describe the answer , then he begin his words using simple and shorts words to clear the answer , sometimes adding a funny example just to grape the attentions of the listeners to attract their mind, then once he finish his answer he used to ask the question if the idea was right and everyone start to bow his head down as a sign of understanding and accepting for the truth , one of the audience approach the mice and asked him once about taj mahal the great Indian white jolwery which considered as one of the seven wonder of the worlds , and the question was is Taj maehl an Indian history or note , then sadhguru waited a minute and said in a very smart way that if anyone weathered you like you don't has built something beautiful the best thing you can do about it is to enjoy rather than saying it built by him so we should not recognized , it is better to just set and imaging it is charming and wondering about how it was built , this a very unique answer from a great person that consider an idol for many around India and in the worlds , because he know that India does not need any more tensions .

((i win first the battle in my mind and then i go and win the battle outside this is how you to gain control))

And that the peace and joy is the best thing to try to achieve in the future and the present most importantly .

Udayeh was listing to this words and he was thinking oh this could be a great way to look up to life and handle the problem Udayeh understood that life more of a journey that is full of joy and experiences a tough which bring within it wisdom and clarity to the human being .

Udayeh got interested about the life of other culture and how they are so rigid , they don't get affect by other option , and bonus they don't get bored they always have something to do with their time

Sadhguru said something very amazing that has getting Udayeh's attention one time , he said the best thing to do is to just set in silence and do nothing and think of nothing , Udayeh thought to himself like why would you be happy if did nothing and at nothing , what is the joy in doing so , many well think the same and it is not wrong to , but if you look at it clearly you will find that being in silence is amazing in Itself , not using your fife senses for a while will make you aware of the world within more , if you close your eyes and block your ears tell what is the different of you from the dead ones , they also can see or hear, it is suddenly dark and silence inside of you , you will start diving at your real inside and inner world , or let me say you mind .

The ability for us to be notice not just what is around us but what is within us is so important and makes wonder what is the mystery behind us .

In the next chapter will be talking about an amazing concept that bring you to a clock the concept of your life , how you face really control , how did your mind came to formulate ,what is the factors lead to your ideology and beliefs .

((It is okay to feel , it is okay to lose it is okay to change our thoughts for a better one , time passes and things changes eve time , so we need to make our life worthy of doing what we love))

karmatic logic

Have you ever heard of the words karma? It is a very common word that HAS been spoken by many, and everyone believes that the meaning of KARAM IS bad and good, or the punishment you receive for the bad things you have done in your life; we will later investigate the true meaning for that word, concept, or whatever you want to call it for now.

Udayeh was one a day walking in a field and suddenly he saw a pique mother and her small babies running behind here and then he saw the dogs other animals parking on this pig family as they enter their area the mother of the pig kept walking none caring about the threat followed by her babies and suddenly something happened , one of the babies stop for a while and lost away from his brothers pigs and he saw that he could just run away to catch his mother pig but he just could do that and instead he ran the other side and lost his way completely so what happen is that the dogs and wild animal took advantage of that and start to move close to him and finally the grab him ,

Udayeh was thinking why would that happen, what would have led to the tragedy for a baby innocent animal, and then he remembered an old saying that if you lose your focus, you lose your line, and that this small animal could have just kept following his babies brothers and would of survived all the way, but the sound of the parking animal and the heart beats of the evens made him lose his focus and led to the end of his life.

And Udayeh kept thinking that this was just a checklist for him, that he should always be so focused on his way during the act.

but what karma has to do with all of this , well **karma as is meaning what it really mean is it mean the action you karma is your actions** , that what **sadhguru** say in his book karma , and state that the action that you make in your life is the karma that set and seeing your destiny and as if you have seen me talk about the pig story as example that if you really did not pay attention to the attentions and steps that you take during your life then your karma or your life event will be not predictable to you , and you be totally lost in your way to the future if you have , so what karma mean is not the punishment you get by god just by getting and doing a bad acts , it is more deeper than that , karma simply mean the way you think also about the event you do in your life ,

let me give a short example just to understand more , let say for example that you have a very smart and beautiful friends in your class or at work , and he has more money than you do and more friends around , you always envy him and think that he is a show off person and you start to hate a lot , and one day he talk to you and told that he want to be your friends and help you out , so that and you say to him responding that you are better than him and he is so rude by wanting to help , then this is your actions and you feel angry , and that is you karma that you have done that to yourself , but now thing of the story like that what if you had something that he did not own , what if he saw in you something that is unique and odd which made him happy or sad , then that is his karma ,

The thing that everyone has his own Karma and if your friends would start to show off and humiliate you then that is his Karma and he is going to live with that .

If start growing that feel of hatred and used to build your reaction then you are making your own karma , every time you fuel your actions with a hate or anger feeling you are somehow and some way making your own **karam** destiny , that how strong and dangerous you feeling effect on your own life , it very important to pay attention to every act and every feeling that we build in our life , we should keep our heart pure and clear from every black feeling that might come in , udayeh was absorbing that when he get to know the reality about how your life pattern constructed with you , it all about how look at other and how you look to the world , what kind of attention you hold inside your body , and what kind of feeling do you formulate inside your body it is the thing that you should really care about , and be conscious about .

Everyone on this plant can really make his own destiny by just making the right decision , so for example if you saw someone done something that makes you so much anxious don't rush to make conclusion about him and start attacking him , try to build a reason or ask your life what could make him do such thing , what are the attention behind , you might find something that helps you to analyze the and once you do so you will really start building you karmatic actions and start to control it even so .

don't let your anger control you , don't let you emotions control you , don't let your imaginations control , but rather than let your mind think and find the truth what help you control your reactions , because some once said that ((that a Man is not a dangerous person a Man is nice and kind person that can control himself and become dangerous when he feel that he is should))

- A man is the person who control his feeling and actions.
- and quietly act upon his plan.
- A man waits for his for the right moment and strike back with unparalleled wit cunning.
- A man dazzles his opponents and destroy their power.
- A man controls his mind and pure his heart.
- A man can be a lion and a flower as needed.
- A man smashes fascism in the eyes of his envious and peers.

TWO
GROWTH AND FLOW

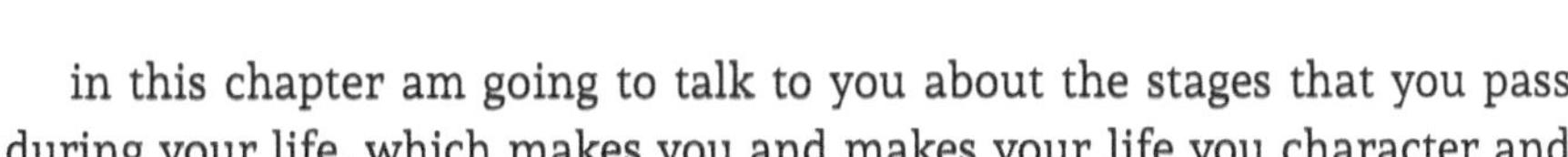

in this chapter am going to talk to you about the stages that you pass during your life, which makes you and makes your life you character and you personality from sperm to dust.

everyone one in your life reach a level of awareness that define him and make him what he is , and that level define .

so udayeh was listing to a man that was called jordan peterson on youtube and dr. jordan peterson said when he was on a t.v meeting life. that you level of awareness can vary from to another ,

first we have the first level of awareness where your awareness is only within the small family or community and country, you only here follow the other attitude and behavior and your , all of you ideology and beliefs and already shaped in you , and main character of this kind of awareness or beliefs that are inside and the that control , is that you have not choose it, but it choose you, you were born with it , in a another way of saying this level of awareness has been formulated with during the 7 years of you living with your family and community were where you were young you start to carefully watched other and especially the elderly one and start to copy them in every action they do , and step by step this level of awareness start to leap into you until you got the program that is now moving , but after that you choose to conjure you next stage of your life with that kind of awareness that you hold within you .

That kind of Awareness is said to be so solid and not easy to change , there are many barriers that help shaping and creating this level of awareness and it is as follows :

Family barriers
Friends barriers

Community barriers

all OF THIS barriers affect that way you think about life and how do you see the word , affect how do you view other.

So the question rise now , what is going to happen when you meet a nether person who is his belief is totally different from you , Udayeh once was coming back to Mysore city , when he was sitting and enjoying a cup of coffee in the morning he decided that he want to meet his friends from Mysore that was called Siddhartha , now Siddhartha was from a another country of Udayeh cause Udayeh was from Italy and Siddhartha was from India .

And when Siddhartha used to talk about his family and his community traditional Udayeh was lasting and hearing something new that he is not familiar with the concept where Udayeh has it inside of his mind , but Udayeh in his mind he was aware that it is okay to have differences with other ,it is okay to listen to other when you are not inserted , or when they are no bringing the familiarity common things to your ears .

There is once concept the or I am going to called ((trayngya)) which mean if something is not running in my flow of interest I don't bother , if something is not enjoyable for me but it is enjoyable for other I don't give attentions or pay part of my time to understand what is the other part is saying , so everyone is drawn in his trayngya thing , everyone is living that if you can watch Cleary what is the other is trying to add to his words from value to stander , someone say the thing that we should do in our life is to spend more effort to absolve everything around us and use what we know in order to help us to expand our knowledge .

My master said to me once hay : don't make conclusions about people , don't use list people that is bad and that is good , don't make them as a lists of your own judgmental tool game , that well bring bad karma to you which that you have to deal with in the future coming on you own.

If you start labeling people that one I like and that one I don't like , then you will start making you world not one , you will start creating your own suffering because no one is good and no one is bad berthing changes with time ,

His brother once gifted Udayeh a nice book called the alchemists and told him to , it was a very famous book at that time and Udayeh just loved the idea . he felt so excited to read it in the morning and look no further the next day Udayeh got that book and sat mooring with a cup of coffee and start to read the book , I have read the book and enjoyed every minute of said Udayeh , the booking is talking about a younger man who travel around the worlds searching for his dream , faces many events and crisis but at the end he manage to complete his goals .Udayeh was so fascinated about reading books , he once heard his master saying that reading books can really change your life and makes you a better person , you just have to enjoy the process each day and night .

One of the best way to train you brain and exercises is to read books daily at least for 20 minutes , Udayeh life become so much rich and enjoyable , he found a vary magic feeling once he read books it just such a amazing feeling , after he finished the book of alchemist he thought to himself that I am going to continue on this habits which has not been so familiar for me .

A book can really be your friends in the dark bight , in the rainy days , and in the cold morning , a book is a master that never failed to address your imaginations and ignore the spark of light inside you with it is content and story , you can really progress by just reading a book once a day , this was the advice of the yogi to Udayeh a yogi who loved his student and wanted them to flourish in their life , his said every time you feel bored just get yourself a book to read a and make it your friends for some time , he will never disappointed you or letdown , he will travel with your to another world of joy and entertainment .

22He said my fellow mate here I leave ten benefits for reading book and that is why I insist on reading book :

1. Reading book can increase your clarity and focus very much and that has been proven in many scientist research in Harvard and oxford , once you ready you brain start to unite it is concentration and make your body in a sharp state , son you should read at least 10 to 20 minutes a day without any distraction or multitasking activity , just block you air from the outside worlds and simply start reading any book you like , this will really benefit you , and you have to do it consistently eve day , if you make this as your habits you will be able to exercise your brain and refresh the brain cell .

1. Reading book give a strong habit that will help to be focus and consisted in your daily life , if you want to achieve any goal in your life then you will be able to manage that very easy

3. Ready book make you discover yourself and your inner side , once you start reading books you will get

4. Reading book will reduce you anxiety , I you have any kind of anxiety then reading book will work on making it reduced and heal it

5. Reading book helps you to build the habits of serving and standing still , he said how come ?

He replayed : once you put yourself to read and keep going you start to find a clarity and abundance inside your self

6. once again he said that : reading a book for 20 min a day will help to set yourself for the rest of the day , this will give a boost for your brain ability to focus and expand its cells and it is clarity by just keep reading books that you like everyday

7. reading a book will help to organize your thoughts and mind , he said and how is that ?
He replayed will : since you are reading your brain is organized because you are exercise it daily and activating your focusing , you brain will be able to grow and become a better machine to help in your life
8.reading a book can really make you discover a new area of life , because e every book behind an author who really brought his life experience to write about , reading a book will be you joy and blesses to your heart and you Soule , you will feel relaxed calm ready to finish your day in the most possible way .
9.the only exercise for brain is reading books , if you want to exercise your body you do exercise at the gym , if you want to exercise your brain you read book for your brain to get better function , clarity and focused on your daily basis duties and tasks in your life ,
That is why most of the mastery people , the Greatest people of all time never stopped this habits of Reading books everyday so they can keep their brain active and ready .
10. second in most of the religions around the world the ideas of Reading Books has been there , like for many such as Christianity , Jewish , and Islam all of the this religious order their people to read books and keep getting knowledge from the booked , the structure of this main religious

even Hindu bodesim and Sikh came via books , so that just tells you how much important is Reading books every day .

I need can keep going on and on with the benefited of reading books but I want you to really get insightful about this once you my friend really start applying these ideas and formula you will really start saying a shift in your life on how to become more committed and Roseland toward your goal and life my friends .

One friend his name was robin Udayeh has meet him and told Udayeh oh my friend i have once small piece advice for you always catch you days and read a magazine or a book early morning and follow this step with a cup of coffee you can boost back you energy and prepare yourself for the day .

Once you wake just mediate or do some prayer wash your forehead with cold water , then follow with the some exercise because you know that your body is a great element of the success formula which I called MBS , YOU KNOW my friends that that is your job to invest in your body and your life too... and UDAYEH said oh that very nice world

From i which someone told me that before .

Of course said UDAYEH ..when you weak up and start exercise your body produce a chemical that called ...... and that give you more energy and make more active .....then after that you go and do your mooring plan task with more passion and commitment to achieve daily .

I am going to give you the formula up next ...

Sleep early ---à weak up early ----àmediate or pray ------à exercise ________ >

Read a book ______>work on your daily project or plan -------

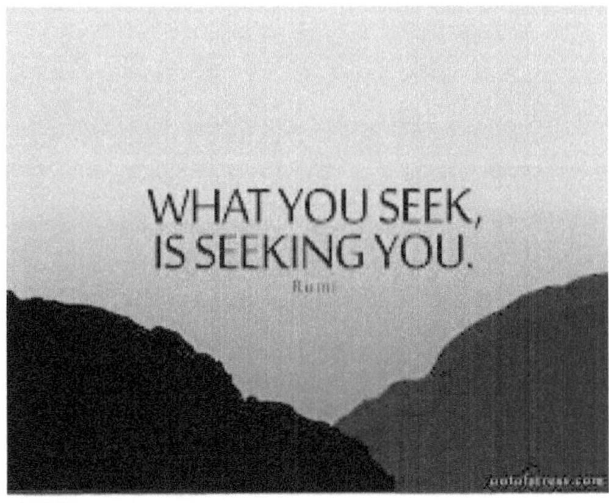

always keep in mind you will be there

things that shows you that you really have grown and expanded ?
How to really know that you are really starting to having a growth and evaluations inside you , well that a very good questions to ask and to talk about .there are many sign that says that you are on your weak to have a spiritual awaken inside it is a very essential and important process and everything is entangling together ,
CHARLESS DUHIGG in his famous book the power of habits says that there is something called the **chain reaction** habits and what does that mean is that there are some sort of habits once you change it will ignite a chain reaction of new habits and changing old habits around it , which is a very amazing thing to learn about my friend

THREE

THE MBS FURMELA MIND, BODY ,SOULE

IN THIS CHAPTER YOU WILL GET INTROFUCED into a very important formula that will help to achieve your daily goal and invest in your life with the most important things ,for you to be able to implement this formula you need to follow it step by step and not neglect any part of it this formula is so important for you to shift your life and start fresh again ,it is a very simple and easy to follow once you start first step , but one thing can help to garmented is to take you into actions , there many problems and barriers that you might face into your life but you just have to know the perfect scheme that will help you overcome this in many times of your life .

Your life need to be set up correctly and in such why that makes you more joyful and appreciate every moment of it , have ever seen a yourself really happy at every moment of your life , but then what is lacking from you that makes you need this , what makes better there are many things you need to work in that will help to improve your way of living and in order for you do that you need to follow some sort of plan or program and committee to it , so you can get the benefits and help that is needed , and here come the MBS formula that I have introduced to you which will make your life better my friends .

All that time Udayeh was listening to his friends joseph talking about this it is very basic my friends you really need to apply this every day at a specific time and then you will be able to get the need result that you targeted at .

His friends Siddhartha said if you really want to achieve this life you need really to commit to the his friend told him how can i shift my life and live a very fulfilled life that brings me joy and happiness to the degree that i feel that i am really doing it right .

t and really wanting to transform yourself completely .

There is a very golden role I this life that apply to every I this life and this role is that if you want TO have something new to your life you have to spark it by action , for example giving something , looking for something , asking , finding , all of this kind of actions will brings what you what once you really what changes into your life .

But what if I could just keep going and manage my potions , what if my goal and road was not clear ? he said .

The replayed the Master then just work one thing , which is clearing your goals , work on three thing to do that .

First you have to know who you are in this life

And second you need to know what do you need from this life

Finally, Why you want to do that

Once you have a Answered all of that then you really can reach your goal and pursue your real life , once you really know the gym that is inside you will shine in the time of life .

But first you have to really work MBS state , which is you mind , Body , Soule , once you really work in thus three elements your life will become much easier to follow in , and suddenly everything will become much closer to you in order to achieve in your life , because how can you really enjoy you beautiful car if you hand are not healthy , how can you enjoy your picture and time with friends and family if your body are not shaped and you don't like you appetency , and finally how can you find peace and power for god if you Soule is not pure , how can you communicate with god .

How to manage your thoughts and ideas that come from your mind daily.

THEN Udayeh walk away and went to play some piece of piano in order to set his mood to calm and enjoy the moment, he starts thinking of what the master said to him about his life and how he can master his own life in way that no one could imagine, how can we be such happy and joyful from the inside just by doing what we love and helping our self and our body.

Udayeh playing the piano which he loved so much made him feel so calm and abundance, there were so much entangled emotions inside, happy, sad , proud , and more ....

if we could just tell our self that one day we will really succeed and we want have to be so worry about our future and just believe strong about that

, then only we can be so convince to work forward , once we start work on our sled and personal development process , we will start really feeling that we are living truly , and we are living our self , as we should do just by taking care of our food that build our cells and body ,and adding to that working out in the early morning to boost out body and active our blood circulations .

this is Avery important duty that we owe out body and we must take It as very series from now on .

Then to continue with our process of personal development and growth we also check our mind , and aim to have a pure and clear mind that we control and get rid of all the bad thoughts and emotions that control us and take advantage of the bad time and setbacks , by doing some kind of exercise we will be able to have a clarity and peace within out self.

Reading books and doing meditation in the morning will help to start controlling or mind and out thoughts , because your mind is very dangerous machine that you have and if you cannot control it you will not be able to live a joyful life because it will always Hurt .

Once upon a time there a man cutting a fruit next to his student and then only the student ohm be careful my master the knife is very sharp .

And then than man replayed it ok it is a knife is supposed to be sharp so it help cut the food easy and without EFFORT, and after 2 minutes the student replayed and said again oh my master be really ...be careful you might cut your finger ...

then the Man said: oh what I have told you it is a very normal to be sharp so that is why we need it .

the insist student said : but it is a really sharp knife .. and the master almost cut his finger.

The master look to the student and said : ok ... I see that you are not really getting the idea .. let me help you with that ... see the knife is very helpful and also it is very dangerous , but that depend only if you have stable hand that what you need to know it is very important to have Avery sharp knife and steady knife and then you will always control the knife and use as you should .

The student look at the master and said ohm .. I get it so the key is to have a steady hand and then you will be able to master the knife .

The Master said yes a steady hand .... And motive that the same think goes to your life once you have a steady control over your brain you will be able to control and control

\

You mind work in such way like the knife they are both dangerous and useful at the same , but it all depend on you how to use them and manage your life , so the master said to UDAYEH ((only a steady man can control his mind and then only he will control his life))

UDAYEH went to his home and he was thinking how you can really work and find balance in your life once you really take control of yourself and in your mind , it is truly magic and charming to just to be able to control your mind .

A man was walking one day near to a river and he saw an old man setting on the edge of the river and stirring at the running water and enjoying the sound of the badger water .

So the man came close to him and said : please can you grace and advice about the truth of having a joyful life .

Old man said : yes , you must first take control of you mind .

Man : how ?

The old man : you have to live every moment as it is and never think about the past and only then you live .

The man said : but it is very hard but I think I will give a try .

Old man said : it is hard because only it is worthy , that is why you have to train your brain and to set and think of nothing every day for at least three month and then you will start to feel some results .

The man said oh ok that sound inspiring and appealing to myself , I must start from today and I will take care of my mind and train it to work me .

Old man : exactly you have to train you brain to work for you not against you and then only you will succeed .

Man : oh right ..thanks a lot for the priceless words and advice .

The man walked away and start to implemented the old man advice and sooner he started to really gain a change in his life, and leave his mind prison .

He only know that intruder to rake control of your life thoughts, decisions ,feeling , and your emotions you have to take control of your mind and that what he have done , ever since then he became a new man with a new mind set , that sat him for the glory and joy .

Only your emotion and your feeling your mind will be reflected in your body , where your physical diminution is the end result showing how did you received the external data from the outside

The physical Dominion

UDAYEH was once walking in the road of India and he saw a guy called mike having funny and telling people about the important of getting a better body that helps you to enjoy your life and feel your young and time .

Udayeh came passed this guy and start to lasting to him while he was saying that you really need to think about getting a better shape ....!! you need to love your body and become a better version of yourself ....then he said I have been thought this stage of my life when I was feeling so lazy and tolerantly my fat body , I use to just set and eat some junk food , until I felt I need really to change myself , I saw an ad on a man sitting in hospital with his family and children around him , while he was in pain , this add got in to me and made really worry whether I am really going to ended like that , and spark a fire inside to really start shifting my life .

Udayeh was really influenced by the man who said it is fine you just need to start by doing small habited to excessive routine in the morning, but that is not only enough you need to really follow that by doing a healthy routings diet that help you to grow it and shift your life

HERE IS THE STEPS THAT YOU NEED TO FOLLOW :

Step one: you need to check your body state weather you suffer from any problem while doing your daily routine or you just are natural do what you do , does your body prevent you from doing daily work and task at your life , do you suffer from any pain or trouble while doing so .

You have to ask someone you know who has experience in body and shape so you can know from where you start ,you need to set you self a program that you need to follow for at least six months and you need to follow it consistency a on a daily basis .

Step two : you need to find the free time that will help doing this program

Food system : you need to know that playing sport without having the healthy food system is useless , because the calories that you will lose in the food system you will get it back from unhealthy food that you might be eating or having .

Third passion : first week of the program is going to be very hard and no enjoyable and especially first three days , so you need really to just push yourself and start doing your life .

Fourth reflect : after you complete the first month you have to look back and check yourself if you really implemented the program steps correctly and if you felt any changes.

fifth growth : so after you check your body and what the results and work that you have achieved you need to start upgrading your program to next higher goal and not just stop at some point.

For the first step is going to be the hardest one , so the master said I am going to give a small example of program , you can start to follow

Six even after you upgrade your body you need to start working on other elements of the human which is also needs. to be take care of .

so after your body is in healthy most peafowl state then it is the turn to look after your mind and Soule , if you mind is not in it is best state then you strong body is not really , think of it like that : if you had a great super car and it is very fast and stronger , but you don't know how to drive , then what is the point if it the master said to Udayeh, so please my dear friend just take good care of the mind that you have , your mind is a very stronger machine , as tony robins says that your mind is the most dangerous and useful tool that you could ever had .

so that why you should really start working on your mind

Seven after you have solved out your problems of your mind and you managed to controlled you need to start working on your Soule and your spiritual part , you need to start having a state of peace and clarity inside which is very useful , and this state starts just by doing certain types of steps that I will help to do .

This states of spiritual awaking:

1. **Find you inner self** : it is a very important steps for any spiritual experiences , where you have to start from the self-first ,before you look around and focus on the outside energy , you should aim at making your mind and your body to work for you , and control your own thoughts and mind and then you will only start to build something within .

2. think positive: don't be so optimistic about life , every time a bad event accrue in your life you need take it as it is and not think too much why it is happening and how it happen ,

Everything is happening for a reason so just be optimistic about your life
,

And think of every event that happened in your life and how you went worried and overthinking of how terrible it is , and then everything went so fine at the end , and it was all in your imagination, as sadhguru says something very strong that 99% of the event and worst expectation that you think of does not happen ,so why waste your time and overthink everything and instead just keep calm and think fast .

1. **Give and receive** : in order for you to start making the world to work for you should attributing some kind of work or shares in this world , you will eventually see that the universe will make everything work for you on the other hand , that is the rule of the being , everything you work on will get back to you in a different form things .

3. **seeking** : one of the most important aspect of any great people and genesis is that they have the urge to search for what is missing or for what they feel it is needed to growth and enhance their work , they always ask for what is not normal and specs everything , measure it, analyses it unite they feel they have something unique to search for , it is very important to search for new experiences and new answer for what you have not been into before , this will make more able to master what you are try to make .

4 .Be present : if you really want to start a new life and path of your own choice then you should really make you self-ready for that , that only can happen by clearing your mind from all the traditional that you have learned before from your societies , your family ,friends and other sources , it is very crucial to pure your heart and your mind first , start from the deep base level , again it is life you are being born again ,

5. communication : you have to learn you self how to be a good communication , not just with the people but how to communicate with the events , problems , ideas and intuition , if an event happen how to read it understand it and how to make it works for you , same for problem and crisis if it happen how not to fall in the trap of fair and stress ,worries and start understand the matter of the problem , how to be able to read all the lines and make the right decision in the right time .

How read the events that are happening in front of you every day , the feeling that you get it is a skills you need to practice on to have it , because it will help a lot in your life once you really understand it .

6.Healthy : if you really want to start you trey spiritual you need to have a healthy body and mind , that will make you ready to receive the right clarity and pure state of mind , anything bad for body from smoking , alcohol, drugs is going to affect your ability to become healthy since we live in a world who is filled with such negative style of life , anything that can get use distracted while we need to function at the maximum level possible.

If you think being healthy mean to have a perfect body and perfect social life then you might be wrong , the really meaning of being healthy is to have healthy decisions , healthy goals , healthy , if your thoughts and your perspective of life is not healthy and not positive then what is the points of having a good body or good house .

7.InnerModeling : it is a new term that you will be introduce to , this term basically helps to manage yourself from the inside , it helps you to become more aware of every aspect of your personal life , your mind , and your states , if you would want to become more aware of what is going on inside you then you should have you self-checked , mentor by your own self not by other**s.**

Set yourself a standard for your actions and for your daily routines , at the end every week give your self-time to analyses your actions the course of your week , and how did you performed looking at the standard that you have set for your self .

Inner modeling is about organize yourself from the inside and bring control to your mind and to your inside behavior , and that is very important because once you have the inner control then definitely you will have the outside control .

Then Udayeh went to ask his Master, then how I can put anything to work? , how I can start creating and building a better versions of myself ? what is the only thing that if I managed and do then I can do everything thing I want and I wish to happen

the Master said:

Organize your mind: if you really organize you mind and only then everything you which can happened.

A well-established mind is very strong state of living, and it intern organize your whole

system, your body, your emotions, and your energy , eve thing will be organized in that directions .

The Master emphases and said, trust that once all of this four dimensions are organized in one directions and you keep it in one state all synchronized together, and then only everything you witch will happened , without even lifting a finger of your hand .

One your four dimensions are united and lined up then all of your life will be in the palm of your hand , you will feel that you are a different human being , you will start to sense everything in new way , every actions you take will be conscious and carefully .noticed your eyes will shine and glow from the signs and magic that will surround you

Udayeh replayed oh will that really touching into my deep Soule sir , I really felt that really already happening inside me , just to be able to leave and have everything you need is the dream of everything fine man but may I ask how. I can really start getting to this stage of my life ? is it really long process ? is it hard to reach there ?

The master said !: I am not going to lie to you ! it is hard and long way but you should that it is really worthy to get there .

Once you really reach to this level you will forget all the stage and hard work that you devoted in the seek of claim there .

UDAYEH SIAD but how I can know that I have really reach there ?, what are the sign that tell me that you are there ?

The master at the top of the Himalaya mountain will you need really to ask you self every day did I really reached there? do I really feel that I am really on the way to master my own karma and my own life? , you will be able to tell by yourself .

There is no really solid answer to that, but you cannot deny the feeling and the beats of your heart that you really evolved , you brain is a very true part of your body that lead the ships , you need really to work on knowing how your brain work ? and what are the nature of your brain ?

Udayeh said what are my brain role in me?

The master said you brain is so complicated in itself that it collect every signal form your sound into your ears , from the image that collected by your eyes , and from the smell going through your noise to the tough from your skins and body and transform all of that into an electric signal that transform from cell to cell until this signal reach to your brains , which will process all of that and start creating the information's that will give a urge to act upon it .

Oudh said : oh my , that is so fascinating all of that is done by this small brain in my head , then how I can neglect this piece of art that our god put inside ? I should really learn more about my brains , you are really opening my eyes this whole journey is start to giving me a new way of viewing the life , I am still younger and humble my lord , I am worth noting without your mercy ,

Everything my lord Allah has given is really to be appreciated and thanked for by us the human being.

WHAT ARE THE ANTURE OF MY BRAIN ASKED UDAYEH?

THE Master said: you brain separated into two area .

1. The conscious area of the brain
2- The subconscious area of the brain
Both of the area of the brain plays a very important role in your life and existed in your body, once you truly lean about this and start knowing how

do they work, you will be able to master your whole body and everything will start to change to your side.

Oudh said: said yes, I totally agree with what you have said, I am really willing to put the work and the efforts that required from me to truly understand.

The master said If you have travelled or heard about the people of Syria in Palmyra where the first alpha where written there you can truly discover more without the human being and the life that has been manifesting there

This civilization has brought so many wisdoms and knowledge to the humanity that has been almost forgotten away.

the maser continue and said that we are still tell now discovering and learning how the old people used to train their brain and bring the best of their life to work their way out during the past , it is really magical if we really can open our eyes and sink with our imagination to depth in to the glory of the past and get the most out of it .

The Thinking Methodology

The Method of Thinking

Brain can is prickle and ONE OF the most tools that human body has so just understand the way it work is very crucial and can help us a lot in the our daily life and in order for us just to understand how it work we need to really know how It worked and how our thought just work during the day .

The human brain is the most evolved brain among all the animal, birds and insects.

Your emotion and thoughts are a results of the information that you have gathered from the world outside and this is your own drama that you have in your head the master said , he went also : and this thoughts and emotions you have , mighty not have any relation with the reality , and if you are having a negative emotions coming from around and you own conclusion about everybody then you will suffer, and this might happening because of the psychological process has been continuing on and on without stopping and that is because you are paying attentions to everything .

You are not able to direct your own thought, and your brain is not well managed and that is four you cannot enjoy your life, your thoughts are just keep coming and coming and your brain is gathering this information from outside and saving these thoughts.

What is happening that what you gather you think that is you, the feeling that happening in you from outside you keep thinking that it is you.

If you saw a door will you say it is you, and then you might thing that I have gone crazy, and that is not true , that is what happening with you . and the problem with that is what happened is that , what you are thinking now has become more important than the fact that you are alive

The Master said: I will give I solution before that you should know that emotional intelligence is not consciously thinking which is mean thinking at the current situation , because this is mean that you are reacting only to the situation and then you are thinking , and that is definitely not the answer ,and paying attentions to the little things around you , if you stop worrying about what has happened in your past and stopped feeling so guilty about it, or you start being anxious about may or may not happened and just start operating according to the right now moment ,according to the current situation , and thing here is the catch , you will train your subconscious mind to manifest the thing that you truly want and desire in your life .

Udayeh said: then how I could be able to control my thought and emotions? how I can focus on what I am doing right now ?

Master said : will my student , sun has come out on time , and planet is spinning on time , and the moon and everything other plan are doing their circle , but you are having a thought that are keeping stressed then the problem is from you.

You have to just focus on the one thing that are you doing right now and leave everything around complete it is own work.

Your mind should take instructions from, and not the opposite, if you could control your own mind then you will be happy, and in order from you to overcome anxiety , so I will give a very nice piece of advice , just watch every thought that enter your brains and do some kind mediation daily for some weeks , and then your anxiety will gradually come down and you will start feeling better .

Udayeh said oh that sound right, I really should try this kind of practice , in order to clear my mind and my thought .

Master: everything in your life happened for a reason and there for you should really understand what is really going on behind the event in your life , andyour role here is to look carefully at this things that happen around , and ask the question why is it happening now ?

You should know everything happened around has a massage to that you should figure out what this massage ,

Here is the sequence:

Event -------à people , emotions(messages)------------thinking ,asking (answered)

THERE IS NO CUENCENDNCE IN LIFE YOU NEED ONLY TO AKS YOU SELF THAT SIMPLE QESTIOSN WHY EVERY TIME THIS IS HAPPING?

WHY AI AM FEELING LIKE THAT?

Master said i will guide to a place that you need to go for witch is a very greater place, where you can really discover yourself, Udayeh: oh that what I am doing, thanks a lot for your advice master, I am really flowed with your knowledge and your wisdom.

The master said it is better for you to go out and seek the knowledge and wisdom that you want never settle here in one land , go the place that I have guided you to and become a better vision of yourself there are many places in this universe that are fall of wisdom and knowledge for inside wealth and joys.

You job is to keep moving and searching for such places, I wish you all the best of luck and blesses for the deep of my heart , I had a great times with I think I was also luck to spend this time with you my dear friends let's all keep in thought and remember that life has no limits , no titles , no names or places , life is just that energy that you spend it , feel it and bring to the world

FOUR

4.MINDFULNESS STILLNES WHAT IS IT ? HOW TO ACHIEVE IT ?

Udayeh went to Chennai to meet his guru (guide) to life , because he wanted to find some answer to his life problem , he wanted to find some answer to his anxiety , he wanted just created a peaceful mind that can really make him feel life and just enjoy every moment ,this is not easy goal to achieve , you must really try everything to even get close to such goal , Udayeh went to Chennai on his next step to follow his master advice who told him to do so , he went to the land of Tamil were could find something could guide him to the truth of the universe and he did find something very unique , just from the first moment he land his foot on the ground of the city , he felt that something magic has happened , he sense a new kind of energy just flouting in the air , that there is one of kind of new rhythm is being played he felt .

He start looking at the people eyes and at the places around , this place he felt has a new kind of meaning to him ,all of that has given a more reason and push to keep on his journey to be more glamour and find more answer to his life , he could smell the ocean from far , because the place he went for was on the beach of the Indian ocean , which just gives more charm and meaning to it , he asked for a place called osha , he was told it is far from here in the city , he saw the people around him very nice and replaying to him in Avery different way of chanting and greeting Udayeh felt very happy to be here , the cars were driven very fast the police men were very chill and easy when handling the work . Udayeh decided that he want to just go visited and check the ocean for his first place and sure he did, he went on his small Rich taxis and drove to the ocean , when he first reached he saw the ocean , and his eyes went shocked when he first saw how big the ocean , his head went blown away by the view and how the ocean is just an amazing creature God Allah , he just felt so lucky to be there .

So he just went there and walked on the beach, the sand of the beach was so clean and shining with it is golden ...., the combinations of the colors between the blue color of the water and the golden color of the sand ...... with the white sky color, just made the view so amazing and breath taking.

Udayeh felt the splendor of the scene and the place that he was in , he eyes popping of his place from the beauty of the what he saw , I think he said : If we were like the ocean we just kept being our self and never change who we truly are , only then we will be solid enough to kept going without life and think of life as a place to just we are have a nice cope of coffee or sweet chat with our friends or family .

If we just set and observe everything around us then only we will be able to just noticed the marvels that are surround us from everywhere ,he just sat on the sand and start to mediate while the sun were just setting , the views where just so breathtaking and the sound of the water was so charming , with the wave hitting the ground at the beginning of the beach, the ocean very big and stronger , with the wind it seemed like as if the it is a message from god the creator that be always watching my abilities .

Udayeh finished his trip to the ocean in the city and decide to go to his room because tomorrow he had a big day he had to reach to the place that he was aiming to go for , the osha mountain in north the country .

Udayeh reached the place of the ash mountain and he saw someone sitting on the edge of porch of the house and looking at the sky , he asked him do you know guru .... , I was searching for him , I need to know where he is .the man raised his head and said you are looking at him , he said oh thanks

Udayeh : oh I am thrilled to meet, I have been told about you

China : welcome here to this blessed place where everyone is welcomed here and received , welcome to the join us , have visited out gem of India , the white marvel gem of India .

Udayeh : do you mean the taj mahal , sorry. I have not but it is really famous around the country all over the worlds, I will visited it soon one day

Chain: yes you should visited It represent the icon of love in India , it was dedicated as a gift from the guy who truly loved his wife .

There are so many lessons we can learn from vesting such place and watching this amazing piece of art that has been made and presented To the world, this piece of art took 20...... years of hard work and dedications to be accomplished by the workers , and to be perfected , this craft , there are many lesson that you my dear friends can extract from this story of the love devotions from this man to his wife , and please take all political and relations and stand as human a side and lesson carefully .

Pure given with no expectation

Loyalty and integrity: when you are building your dream you should be .....to what you want to do in your life ,, if really hold on to you want to accomplish everything will unfold for you and you will magnifies what you truly want in your life , have a pure tensions towards the art that you are crafting is heavily

FULL DEVOTIONS AND COMMITMENT: keep doing what you love un your journey and never stop at any points of life in order to achieve it is

PASION: the real crafts that are very few in this world have took a long time to achieve and lots of dedications and hard work with pure heart and body passions

LOVE AND JOY : if what you want to achieve does not bring you love and joy to the depth of your heart , then it is not pure it does not represent you from the inside , you should focus on doing thing that fill yourself and your body with peace and deep love and joy , things that shake from the inside out and really move you ,if your goal does not bring charm and glamour light to your Soule , because that what it spouses to do , should really be abandoned in you are doing .

there really a methods for life you can follow this advices that i am going to throw on you and you will never get lost in lost again ,

there is always a way to mastery

=

1 – Go Big be limitless : Thing to know about you brain function that master said once you start knowing how it works the you can actually work on expand your brain activity limits, with so many study my two dear son that have shown that it is possible .

Don't get affected about what other might say or think about you , and always build a steady steel focus on your life and yourself , what inside is what matter my two dear friends , the only big mistake we do at the very early stage of our life we always tend to value other opinions about us , we really should not do that , we should be more concerns about what is going in our life .

Once you master your own self the magic will happen, the moment you manage your own problem and your own life style you will be able to transfer not just yourself , but you will also transfer other people life too .

You know that the Taj Mahal which is a mausoleum complex in Agra, which one of the finest work of the Mughal architecture, a unique art that has been crafted on this land, which represent the pure love and human gains in devoting their life to build wonder my son.

This work has been so approached and brought joy and charm to everyone who has visited, just to enjoy it to shake the inspiration inside and help to make everything just magical and glamour.

Life is inside your dream and love

2_ Life System : you should know that how you start your day m determine the rest of the day , and how do you manage your all life morning days will determine your life , is not this so incredible , you have to work on your morning habited , stop surrounding to your daily lazy routine , and blame other for your life .

Udayeh said oh that is really tick in the heart of me , this words are truly strong , I have always been so lazy and have no time fixed , I always spent ,my time on things that very small and doesn't matter .

Alan oh right , managing time has been always a challenge for , I will start with a plane to fix my time and then suddenly out the blue I start seeing my self-backing up and wasting time , ii think I have problem in my self-discipline , it seems like it is harder than I have thought .

Will I am happy that you guys are starting to know your first line of the problems, because knowing the problem is the first step of the soloing , since you guys are suffering from that you should that formulating a habits usually takes about 20 days to start sink in inside your brain , and then it will become a part of your daily routine .

So my advices to you is like that build a habits set a time line of 20 days , and keep forcing yourself to do that , and you will find that after t weeks of and consistency it will become a part of your life

You know habits lobs are the cycle that you pass through when you pass during your daily routines, this habits loop are printed inside my friends , and you know it is very important to understand , and how it works , when are repeating something over time a habits will start to formulate inside your brain and it will be printed inside you as you are performing you daily work , that habits are consisted of three stages making it like process which takes about 20 to 30 days to be installed inside your subconscious mind , once this happen the real dangerous is that you will start doing this habits without you being conscious about .

Habit loop:

The habits loop has been studding by many researcher in Harvard and scores , and all of the studies has shown that this habits have a very large effects on our life , and the choices we make and decision that we do .

Habit Loop

And only you can change you bad habits and healthy one, don't you guys want to be so successful and fulfilled such like the Taj Mahal Architectures , and have the habits of success and greatness , the habits of legendry figures , who were able to create their own habits of winners and mastery , that why I am emplacing on habits because it is so erring to have good habits .

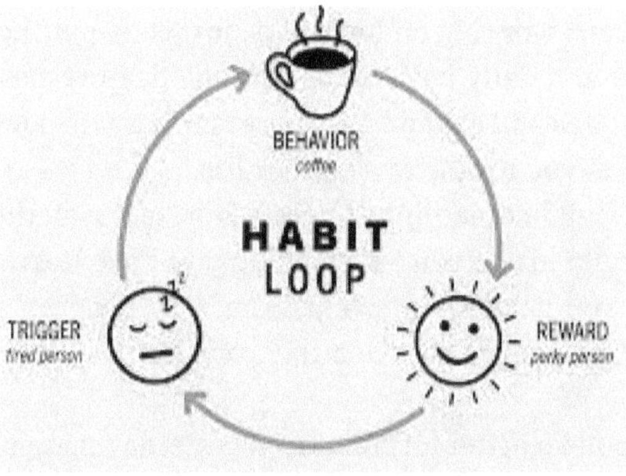

Habite Loop

success habits will attract success routes and it will attract success people and friends, and will eventually attract successful result the master said.

Udayeh well that really sounds interesting and mind blowing, but how ? .....How we can changes how bad habits that control us and come with a new one Master ? How can we know which habited and bad and which one are good

that is good questions, glad you asked master said , will it simple , find any habits that put away from focusing , or makes feel stressed .

once you really build a habits of genius you will see that no matter how you do , no matter how you have been suffering , it will all goes away to the string and passion during the road until we reach what we devote our life for .

3-Build your genius character :

You can all always find something genius about you, everything you do you can turn into genius my friends, he said you know that, stupid people do thing they don't like , and smart people do thing they like but genius people do thing they love and they are good at , so my friend set your mind correctly and make yourself in the right place to growth and explore different areas of your life .

Always try to growth and expand your will power, and there are many ways for you to expand your will power, by train your body and do daily exercise this will help to improve your brain capacity to functions and will always make ready to handle new challenges .

Udayeh yes that right I can manage that with new ideas and plan , I think I need to start working on my brain , just start putting yourself in the discomfort zone in a daily basis until you one day overpass your fair and your challenges , this will expand and increase your will power in a way that will be so useful to you for the rest of Your life .

You need to build something that is really tell something about you , build what is really inside you , everything you have learned from anyone before around , you need to remove it from your memory and create your own story , the time has changed and the world can not be the same for your life .

You need to build a better formula from yesterday that meet your life and fix your struggles and put you on the right track to chase your true goal .

((handle you self to your own the deep sound inside that has been set by the force of the universe and let you heart guide you in the mid of storm, learn how to dance in the rain to able yourself to handle the battle when it happens, the truth is always inside you, you only know the answer to your own problem))

The master kept on going with words descripting the beautify of art, Taj Mahal !! just tell me how could not fall in love with such an antique piece of art came from the results of unparalleled creativity and mastery, this love represents a pure gift from the deep heart to other person, maybe it is just not a piece of art but it is a piece of legendary and mastery.

Udayeh and his other friend who came with him just start thinking of this and then start thinking how could be the master of their own life, and that they should learn the deep lesson of this piece of art.

Udayeh said: I think we all can really build our own peace of art, and master our craft work, when we really put our heart and passion in what we are doing.

The master: I really want you all to focus on the goal that you really want to do in your life and just work with a professional dedication that make your design work an ideal way which bring proudness and given your utmost effort and energies that present you the deep master piece from the depth of your Soule.

And by that, I mean make everything you touch a piece of craft that you really feel satisfy and proud of, make every goal in your life.

4-Set your goal and your purpose:

When you have a goal and purpose in your life it will launch to achieve the impossible and will lead you to don the marvels that you put you in the history.

Look at Steve job he has built the iPhone and it tell now still dominating the market, he keeps doing what he should do, and never settle in to plan for the future.

But how can we find our goal Alan said, well you have to look deep inside your life, what are the think that have made you what you are today, this are the you super power the master said.

All the think that you fair, once you be able to over passed, it well become your super power believe me, someone once said don't say how but rather start saying, what and why, this are. Avery Q group words that will unlock your potential skills and set of tools for you to reach you genius life.

:

SOME ONE ONCE SAID ABOUT TAJ MAHAL:

oh, this white piece of marble that shine in the day light and reflect hues for the moon light and sunlight together.

and it four most charming identical facades that rise above the air with it is apex and chamfered corners that all incorporating smaller arches.

the majestic dome , which reaches a height of 240 feet at the tip of its finial , and it is surrounded by four lesser domes , this acoustic inside the main dome cause the single note of a flute to reverbrerate five times .

the interior of mausoleum is organized with low -relief carvings and semiprecious stones

therein are the cenotaphs of Mumtaz Mahal and shah Johan, those false tombs are enclosed by a finally wrought filigree marble screen.

beneath the tomb, at the garden level, lie the true sarcophagi, standing gracefully apart from the central building, and at each four corners of the square plinth, are elegant minarets.

((. the Mughal emperor who Masters minded this Marvel was a very much in love, as a symbol of this devotion to and adoration to his wife, Mumtaz after her death he committed in 1931 to the construction of a monument to like the world which has never seen before.

one is so extravagantly sensational staggeringly inspirational and structurally exceptional that all onlookers would understand the depth of this man's affection as they experience all it is splendor.it does something to my heart when I look at it , staring at the marble façade that glimmered in front of you , and just seeing that Taj Mahal is an execution of the intellect , it is also a resurrection to the spirit , it wakes even the numbest person up to what we as a human creatures are capable of producing))

FIVE

MASTERY IS WHAT YOU NEED ? HOW CAN WE MASTERFUL ?

Master your work :

Udayeh came the next morning to his friend and said we should go and visited our master get the, his friends said yes, we should, lets waste no time and begging out day with more thing to achieve.

The two of them went to trip to Rome and they both though to them self to take the train to get there so that they can really sense the journey length and time.

This journey needs to take at least 15 days on average but no matter how the decided to do that in the sake of taking the efforts and make it worthy feel and know where they are travelling to .

As those they have reached to Rome this old beautiful city , which is filled with architecture and old building and houses form the time of the Romanian , both of them wanted to discover Rome , Udayeh and his friend Allan , they were so excited to go their because they have been told that there is a man there that have a deep pure amount of wisdom and helpfulness that they can gain and grasp from his .

As they have reaches Rome they started to feel the bold pressure and the heart beats from the fact that they have reached the place

They landed their and went to from the stations to the bus station and their they started saw the city and the people around , well it was a very noisy place but it was well organized .

There was a taxi waiting outside for them just to go and reach from their destination, they rap their bag and went to the nearest taxi , the started hearing the taxi driver speaking in Italian language saying hay you want. A taxi .... the were able to understand him from the signal and his head that he want them to ride with him , the went to him and he star to welcome them .

Driver : where you are heading ?

Udayeh : we are heading to ....

Driver : right I know the place I shall be driving there then will reach in 30 min .

The two were happy to land safely and arrive to the place

Once they have reached to this old place in the middle of Rome , they felt so blessed and happy to be there and reach their distance in the right time , the stop at ancient wall and walked for five minutes when they finally saw a long tower near a hotel were supposed to be , and finally a man came to them and said are you guys looking for the .... they said yes and they kept going ..... then they keep moving and he said let me show you my friends this places that you would so much want to see .

First you have this tower which has been built on the century , and also you it is a very attraction spot for thousands of visitors every month it has the magic of the indigenous civilizations who have lived here .

Finally the reacted to the colosseum and the arch of Constantintine .

Work of art

As the Eiffel tower is to Paris, the silhouette of the Flavian amphitheater is to Rome .

The largest structure to be left by the Roman antiquity, the colosseum still provides the model for the sports arenas – and it presents day football stadium design is clearly based on this oval Roman plan.

The building was begun by Vespasian in AD 72, and after his son Titus enlarged it by adding the fourth story, it was inaugurated in the year AD 80 with a series of splendid games. The Colosseum was large enough for theatrical performances, festivals, circuses, or games, which the Imperial Court and high officials watched from the lowest level, aristocratic Roman families on the second, the populace on the third and fourth.

Beside the Colosseum stands the almost equally familiar Arch of Constantine, a triumphal arch erected by the Senate to honour the emperor as "liberator of the city and bringer of peace" after his victory in the battle of the Milvian Bridge in 312. Lines are long and move slowly, so you can save time by joining the Skip the Line: Ancient Rome and Colosseum Half-Day Walking Tour and have a knowledgeable guide, as well.

You were brought here so you can sense the old city of the Rome , and feel the really history of the city , it is a very remarkable place , where many civilisation has been carried out here , and especially the Roman empire , which dominant the world .

The keep moving untilled they reached an old place looked like a big mosque it was so unique and beautiful from the outrode , it was made of white marble , there was a man waiting outside , he received him well and he had smile on his face , he said he how are you doing over there ?

Udayeh and his friend replied oh we are doing just fine , we are happy to meet dear friend Oscar if I am correct .

The man yes that is correct I am Oscar; I am happy to meet you too.

He was smiling and had a big smile on his face, he invited them to go inside so they can get some rest.

I am very delayed to have here the man said. I think you are both tired from the trip , so please find you self a room inside and tomorrow I shall see you on a new day , I want you both to wake up on the right time , exactly at 4 AM

WELLBEING

((You are not a number you are a universe, so go ahead and chase your dream life and invest in yourself, no one has told you that but you are a king of your time, you are the right one to ask advice from and to rub to in the rainy day and at the dark nights)).

Many of us think we will fail even that we do all the hard work, but suddenly we make out of nothing, we just raise and shock everyone around, we are start in the night and we are the reason the world is being rub)).

Next day, both of Udayeh and Alan woke on time and apprised the day from its beginning, the man who is had to be their GUID yogi in the alley of old Rome is waiting for them to start their new journey in the old street of Rome, where everyone seeks such experience that allows you to discover and disclose new areas in your life .

Both of Udayeh and Alan woke on 4.am in the morning before the light and before the birds start twitter in the edge of dawn and dusk ,the Room of both of them where on the second floor , both of them where sleep yet because of the travel they sat on the room balcony waiting for their yogi friend to come , the view from the room were dark , there was nothing to look or capture , they were both sitting on a couch , they start to wonder if he is really awake , or he is just still in his bed .

After a 20 minutes of waiting the clock starts to approach 5 .am in the morning , finally they start to here a footsteps coming to the door , there patience has reached a long stage of silence and boredom .

((if you think you are happy with your life, then why do you keep wandering in the sunset hours and in the late evening of the night, are they thoughts and signals from worlds far away from you, or they are just a dream from the childhood that you have always think about.))

They heard the sound of the knocking on the door and they turned, it was the Master Oscar himself, saying good morning to both of you, I am glad that you are both awake just in time I want you both to follow me to the next room where I will show you a nice splendid place so please come.

They both followed him after they thought they will not see him, he took them to a very medium sized room in the end of the floor, they both entered the room , once they look they were shocked of the how beautiful is the room and how it is so charming and breathtaking , there was so many decoration on the wall , there was an ancient archaeological panels that represent the history of Rome , and another paint on the wall from the other side of the thinkers and philosophers for the days of the heroes and immortals .

There was also an old decoration from the old Romanian architecture that juts take your eyes away .

The man said you know desire the war for the chair and fights between the human being , the human being has shown that there is a part inside him that is always majestic and charming , his way of representing his pain is just amazing , the Man invited both of them to set on the chair in the room so they can look easily to the art is surround them from all sides .

((The craft inside you need always a time and dedicated love and work so you can be presented to the worlds, look deep inside of you and just close your eyes, look with your heart only , you shall find some sigh and call to guide you to the right direction .))

Both of the man sat old wooden chair, that you can feel that it is from the old days of the great Romanian civilization where there is a captivating luster and a pulse from the past connected with the present, and under their feet they could feel the carpets it was very well designed, the Red carpets stretched across the floor of the Room and decorated with golden stripes that gave it a magical look which take your eyes right away .

Both of Udayeh and Alan were astonished by the beauty of the scene and the mighty work of art, as if they lived in this time,

The man said I want to bring you from the first day on this place so I can show how amazing the work of human being can be , I wanted to make you inspired by the creativity and the perfection in skills and work , also to feel that and believe that there are no limits to your potential .

Udayeh: said yes that is so true , I already feel that I am in thought with the old majestic time that has passed on this place , we really appreciate that we were able to visited this place .

Alan nodded his head and said : I think we should always take the creativity of other as a thing to be inspired be and never limit our life to ordinary and mediocrity .

The man: well said , now I feel that you guys are on the right direction of the your own great journey .

While they were talking about that, a man came and open the door , he was holding a plate of cup , a silver cups that filled with old black tea m which is a just an old traditional drink form the past taste of authenticity and deeply .

since we are staying here and getting our mind shifted into new dimensions of creativity and genius that are located inside everyone of use ,

my call for your my friends is to try to set the new life and attitude of winner ,how can you dream big if you your plan are small .

1. aims at the top :

Always when you dream of becoming the hero of you own life and the hero of you loved one, you should take a micro risk of new studies challenges and hit the line of fear , you should never underestimate yourself under any situation , keep moving step by step utile you build the tower and statue of greatness and business , many of us don't dare to dream at least because they already have a mini mindset of value and appreciation for their self .

Their an amazing saying by someone a really know that goes like this: ((if you know that you don't fail , how big you dream)) , that a wonderful words to set the goal for your true big life and let you just move ahead with your dream, and growth the small seeds of success and love inside within the night , days , weeks ,months ,and years ..... if you just aimed your weapon towards the starts then at the least results you will go above the mountains pick and beyond exceptions.

Make your life the kind of life that you would wish for you kids and family, the one that you would wish for your loved ones, if this is your life then why you are attaching yourself with other thoughts and opinions , dare to invent and to create the best aspects of the life and joy inside . here is a small poem and want to humbly cite for you:

Be the captain of your journey ......be the leader of your nations

Be the master of your life ...... be the guide of your Soule

Be the only version of you ...... be the number one in your

About this amazing and exquisite work of art that you are surrounded with , it is here just to shift your imaginations and transform the way you see life , all of the beauty item has been made of an arms that is creative and bold that has dared to dream and move on with its own dream .

They just could not get enough from looking and scanning the room, they have not seen such a fabulous design and art in one Room, the look up to catch the roof which was made of white marble painted in light cyan white, a dashing that takes an impressive semi -circular shape splendor to the view , its beauty and splendor , as if you were looking at the clear sky outside .

the Man said I just want you to enjoy here and have a wonderful experience that make you inspired in way push your imagination to the limits.

both of Udayeh and Alan sat in the room in their place, enjoying the beauty of the room and had their cups of tea, they will never forget such a pleasant experience.

I have never seen such a beautiful design and creativity before, Udayeh said, well you have to be so lucky and special to witness such experience at these days, I will always be blissful and thankful for you sir to allow us to come to here.

you are right Alan said, I think we are truly lucky to see this mastery piece of art, I am going to call, I really could live here forever and never get bored of this amazing architectural master piece.

I am really honored to have both of you here the man said, I have been whitening for you, I know it was a long journey from India it Italy, you guys are really lucky, you got to see Taj Mahal and now you are here in the street of Rome, the land of the most famous and greatest empire of all Time .

inside the work of art

4 A.M LAUNCH UP:

i have always was fascinated about waking up early before anyone move and open his eyes , I wanted really to introduce you to the new rhyme of life , and which is the rhythm of flowing with the nature , I need you to set with me after a while outside in the balcony , so we can witness the magic of the early morning , at this time where all the genius and legends used to be awake , where they use to connect with the super power of the universe using different kind of methods from the payers to meditation and to the slave , at this time so many magic happen and so many wisdom and clarity a one person can get from .

Udayeh: well I have been always told that there is a miracle in the early hours of the day I used to sometime wake up at 4 AM and just set and mediate with myself and start to plan for the day , but I could not keep this habit forever , I am really parrying that this routine could be my only routine for the rest of my life

Alan: yes true, I guess we need to work out self out to be the best version if out self and just do whatever it takes to build out magical moments in this life .

My rule for you in life is to plan your day early morning and it is better to be from 500 AM in the morning so you receive all the positive energy that the universe send to earth so that every can get a chance to receive and enhance his daystar, it is very important to be under the sun light after 20 moment it is raise , the medical science has proven of the important of the sunlight for human being , anyone who can follow this early morning and get his time right to wake up on 5 AM and start his activity , will feel so much energy and happiness that will push him get his work done by far than any other person .

After you wake up you should start do some spiritual calls or prying as it will connect you with the creator or the force of the universe , and your Soule will be in piece and pure for the day , you should follow that with any kind of meditation to clear you mind and reach the level of conscious that you need for your for your own to set you self for the day , once you finish with this two steps you will feel that you have a great super power to practice any work or task that you feel you need .

I want both of you to follow me to the outside to the balcony are where I need both you to set with me because the light is about to hit the shadow and dark outside, in the silence of the dark of the early days we will be more committed to achieve what we never could, in the line of the In front battle we will see the light of hope and joys.

It was almost dark, and there was no sign of light , everything's was quite , and there was no movements outside . both of the three sat outside and , there was a wooden chair that was made of an old Italian trees it was very old and heavy , it had blanket on top green one and one is orange , both of Udayeh and Alan sat and start enjoying the moments , the clock almost hit 5;30 and then the a small sound of birds babies started to hit the air, it was little bit cold , but both of Udayeh and Alan were enjoying the moment , Udayeh said that is so beautiful and charming everything is so quiet and peaceful , I wish I had done there long time before .

There was a sign of small garden with so many trees form the balcony , and river on the other part little far , Alan said I am really feeling that it is a blessed times ,for us to be here and sit in this place , please notice the master said , it is now a very beautiful moments that will start to come , both of the Udayeh and Alan listen carful, and it was just minute until a golden line started to rise for the river side , and the sky turned into white and blue , the river start to reflect on that and It is colure start to shine , the master said I brought here to witness the rise of the life , the rise of the plans earth where you will see that everything is not what you had seen before please look carefully intron of you , it was a moments until the sun light started to hit the sky and the moon was still glowing in the space given the nature a beautifier combination of it is aspects .

While the sun was reusing, and it is white light was coming beside the lake the sky stated to light up and there was so much energy just flowing everywhere, I am really blessed and feeling joyful just to be able to feel these sensations of clarity and blesses for the mother earth, all of the cycle of life has been given us to refuel our self with power and energy for the day.

I really need this in my life, it the answer to most of my problem in life, ever since i have been losing time and ideas that i could have been execute really in my life Alan said , the man said yes you not too late to start fresh again all you need is just a great one start to rebuild your life and re build you Karma as my great teacher said :

((your life is your karma, and your karma is your actions, and you only need to manage yourself from the inside and you will flow and shine to a whole new level of awaken and mastery to be able to catch up with all of your dream and mission in life))

It was a very great word by a great man that I do very respect and honoree him , and I blessed to know him , I send my love and blessing to you friends , I believe in you that you will one day reach you top of the mountain and feel proud of yourself , you have to know how to control your life , because you are the only one responsible for your life , and are going to have to make decision to decide what you are going to be tomorrow , because no one will left a finger for you or dedicate his life for you to get up every morning and change your life , you are the only one who need to stand for what you want . that is a very powerful worlds I am touched deep down Udayeh said ,I guess we the painter of our paint ,we are the artist of out play , and we are the director of our own movies

((A man will always get up every time he try , a man a will always seek new ideas and a plan for his life , a man will always strive for rising up, it does not matter how you many time you feel , it matter that when you fail you get and fight for your dream)).

Alan: yes will said Udayeh, I guess that we are the writer and author of our own life , so why don't we just write a good brilliant genius master piece story , that we will be pound to tell to our grandchildren one day when we pass the time .

The sun started to rise more and it light had just speeded across the sky and the surrounding , the sky color took a very magical eyes taking color ,and the air was very cold and fresh like heaven , the green trees were lined up across the garden and the birds were making its twitting sound across the sky ,the orange color of the sun disc were coming out at the horizon and there was some sort of massive energy coming every one of the man and two artist and entrepreneur feet it , the man said please juts look ahead of you and take a wander at this miracle that is habiting In front of you , I wanted you to take advantage of this splendor moments and give yourself a gift of life time to see this scenery as it havening now .

Udayeh feel very active and in state of peace from the inside as if my life were so clamoring, I really feel my eyes sparkling and running around this phenomenal event of the nature , my mind is in state of clarity that I wish it last forever.

ALAN : yes that is true , it is true miracle a piece of heaven that has been presented to us from the creature of the universe , we really need to just appreciate this early hours of morning and start to include it in our daily routine , there is a strange sense of every floating in the air , everyone I guess can sense it , it is just astonishing .

light of the path

((Finding your dream is a trip is a journey it is not a choice in an early life time, once you start finding something to help serve the world, growth, and fills you wit hipness and joyful then you should that you have reached to the geniuses and legends side of life that you have always been looking for start living your life like a superhero and a president of your own nation))

((Only true magic happen when you put all of the three elements together your true desire towards your gold, your love and passion into the works and finally the picture of your goals becoming true))

SIX
FOLLOWING YOUR DREAMS

While the time started to hit the 5:30 the sun took it is light orange color and the sky turned mix of blue white and orange colors , the ground view from the balcony were such a slandering fascinating scenery the , the man said I wish now to just take one moment look and then close your eyes for 2 minutes only , then start imagining yourself fully happy and fully rich and satisfies , just keep thinking of the things in life that make you happy and gives maximum amount of joy and pleasant , try of pent another thought of fear or complaining and just take along deep breath in and out fill your chest with pure early morning air and start imaging yourself concurring the world .

Once you finish then please draw what you have saw and felt on piece of paper or note book and keep it with you the man said, I need to keep doing that for the next 20 days tell you leave and before you go to sleep and need to take five minutes of meditation wish will enhance to clear your mind and set you up for the day , this process of morning and evening will make you ready to build a genius plan for your future and will help to achieve what you have always wanted in your life .

Think about three thinks deeply and without any kind of detractions and source of angry I want you to put your love and joyful in inside you when you start asking yourself this deep three quotations , because it is very important before you do anything plan or mission In your life to have an solid answer to this three questions what why and when ......this three W SET OF Tool will make more focused and aware of your own tack , beside that it will build you exact blueprint of your life plan which every human on earth needs this process to have a map that can guide him in his long journey

1-What do you want to do and become?

Before you start you journey and you set your life plan you should know what are the things that you want to do in life, you should know the following:

- What do you want to become in the future?

- What kind of servers and work you will create in the future?

- What is the purpose behind your work?

- What is the standard and values the?

2-Why do you want to become and do that?

- Why do you want to create such things.?

- Why do you want make this plan?

- Why this service is so valuable and important?

- Why do you want achieve this goals?

3- when do you want to start and reach?
WHEN you want to start the plan?
When you will expand and progress your size of your work
When do you want to make more plane?

((So, remember that the main things you need to do before you start working on your life mission you have apply the wx3q methods which is the what, why, when questions which you ask yourself these questions before you start doing your job or any services that you want to do in life , this questions are very essential for clearing the mission for you in life a to know where you are going))

view for the artest

((Life is a chance for you to flourish and become the highest possibility of joy and being, it is chance and opportunity for you to give and race to the worlds, you are not a number you are the master of your own piece of art, be lovable joyful and make you choice always a one that brings you happiness and heathens.))

Remember that every world you say matters, and you have mission in life and purpose that you can puree , once you can dimity this mission your life will become much more meaningful and attracted to you , and you will start to shine and rise like Big starts in the space or maybe like a Galaxy in the universes , so always remember this three thing love you self , care ,growth , protect you self in this journey , because if you don't know one will

,surround yourself with people they love add point out your mistake to help you corrected not make feel good about your mistakes.

There is a good saying that goes like this: ((show me your friends and I will show you your future)).

Both of Udayeh and Alan where inspired and in state of awaking, their spirit were lighting and their Soule were glowing , I have never been in such relaxing and hindering place , I really felt that my life is in my naked hand and my life Udayeh said , I am really making the best quality time of my life , I am feeling that I am on the right track to hit my goal of life .

Yes that is true Alan said ,once I felt that my life is lost and I have no goal in life , and now I found out that my life has been always meaningful but I was not looking enough toward the right direction .

After you have experienced this blessed moments at that early movement of time , you will always know what to do in life and what to ask for when you find yourself in the mid of actions the man said , you should always set you mind right and your body in the best shape every so you can have the ultimate combination every , so remember to take care of your body it is your responsibility to do so , here is my tips for you to have the best shape and physical state that you could have , in the early morning get you self and give you self a 5 to 10 minutes to meditates or to do some prays as that will help you to clear your mind and set your body for the day , then you should after that make some body movement to increase the blood circle and push your body to work better , by just doing some running , or walking in the nature or any other type of movement activity you will have you self-activated and you energy will be on a high level , once you move and excursive your body will very soon produce a chemical inside you from your brain that will push you to the limit and will give a higher ability to start you day and finish you tasks and work in a deep quality and accuracy .

And your brain will be ready to take on the next task , after you have finished the second part of the mooring of exercise and body movement part ,you now should move to the next part , after you have set yourself for the day you should give you self a higher productivity time of a two hour not less than one hour , where you start to take on your challenges and daily plan , you must at that time eliminate all kind of distractions and barriers that might catch you attention from the outside environment such as electronic device and people around you , so that you could have the best quality time and work to make you task and future plan on time

At that time, you should think of one or two thing that you want to achieve and build in your life that you really

Launch yourself 4 AM :

Pray à meditate à imaging yourself succession and
completing all the steps à work out, exercise, body movement à
cold shower à reading Books à Plan a take without any
distraction à communicate with quality people à Pm recheck your work
Follow this this process at the beginning of your days so you don't get
lost , it is very important to start with success and end with success habits
because this is how you train your brain to set up it is software human
program . the studied s showed that you probably to end your plan the way
you have started which mean that you will it is very important to start very
strong to have the ability to end in the same watt, also remember that once
you start a task it is very important how the way you end , this is about
your willpower , one of the things that increases your will power is the way
you end your work or plan , this will increase your awareness and your
willpower in your daily life routine , your start your day with active state of
mind and high tension to complete and challenge your day on the other
hand at the night before you sleep you should say I am tired and depressed
it is fine because I had a long day and I have done so many activates , this is
very wrong and will make you almost destroy your mindset and the way
you end you work , but rather you should be relaxed and happy and excited
about the next day in which mean that you need to train yourself to not
surrender to fatigue and depressed , use some time meditate even half an
hour before you sleep and just don't think of anything and how went your
day , weather it was a great day or a bad one , meditation will make your
mind clear at night and will help to just settle in the circle of peace.
Somehow you have to interrupt this circle of negative thinking by adjust
yourself to a new way of self-talk , ask your brain to stop that and start
produce a positive thoughts , because it is very known that you become
what you think you are , your become what you focus at , that is why you
need to shift your thought towards the right direction .
Here are the benefits of mediation before you sleep just for at least five
minutes :
1-it will make sleep and rest very good and release your mind from any
negative thoughts that you might had during the day
2- it will let you sleep fast and easy

3- it will organized your thoughts and make you focus on the important one , also meditation before you sleep at night will allow to be ready for tomorrow to finish what you have started and keep going focused solid and more powerful .

4-miditation before you sleep will work the way the morning meditation to set your brain to be trained to be relaxed and less worried about the day or yesterday event or problem wand will allow you to focus on the solutions not the problems during the day

5- mediation at night before you sleep will increase you well power to do the small activities you want to do before you sleep such brushing you teeth and organize your table , set your goal for tomorrow , drink water , take a cold shower all of well help for smooth getting ready for sleep and calm you up , and will increase your well power .

6 -meditation before you sleep will help to get a clear dreams and thoughts while you sleep ,for you to noted and writer it after you wake up in the early morning , since son many have shown that brain does not stop working after you sleep at night but rather it keeps functioning , Kwik says that all the problem you have though on during the day the brain at night keeps on to find the solutions for it , so it is better at early morning to write down what you have seen in the dreams .

7- meditation before you sleep will work on

Enhancing you state and your mood, which will make you more focused and solid within you , you will be able to finish your day in the most perfect way in a calm ultra-state of mind , rather than just to spend your last time of your day like the rest of people by bring worried and stressed about what you have done and received today from your work and times with other people , and getting difficulties trying to sleep and probably having a nightmares , so why not meditate before you sleep to help you calm your anxiety and bring relief to your mind and you're your body .

8 Lastly meditation before you sleep will help to improve your body health and your mental health since it will allow you to get a deep long amount of sleep so you can be ready for the next day plans and goal to jump on and smashed , that why my friends a decided to spend time on this small habits that really worked a lot for me during my life , so I can take control of myself and my day, most of people just do mediation at the morning only but now you will take it to the next level and meditate before you sleep which will remind your body and your mind to be always relaxed and calm and never be affected by other and by you day to day problems or

barriers .

I loved this methods before we sleep ,I have always there was a problem facing us at night Udayeh said , that is a very huge benefits right there for meditation you have tension for us sir , really appreciated you wisdom and your talk that has open up the luck for our life , it is really strange how we have the chance to always growth and leverage our life standard and routine ,with just a small steps and slight changes we could have a huge impact on out self ,I used to always get a long stressing time before I get to sleep and never had an idea that this could be because of not clearing my thoughts and worries before I sleep .

Yes I guess you are right Alan said , my self-need to implements such routine and methods, I guess this all have to do with my old habits that I need to change and adopt to a new life style that pay me back with a good results . it is never too late to do so , I guess it is never too late to start changes your life style towards a better and a more efficient way of receiving the problem of life .

Yes that is very true my two younger friends I really enjoyed giving you this time , you guys are true amazing , please be always stronger and courage while taking your day to day decision and always check you habits there is a greater saying by my friends that I will never foregut which goes like that :

((you don't decide your future but you decide you habits and your habits decide and create your future))

Get you self a decent system before you go to bed and forgive every one that hurt during the day or the week, don't carry negative emotions and negative energy for the rest of your life

Rome((Take control of your life and be the creator of your life, never give fighter to get a great life that brings you happiness and joy, the magician of your life, be the driver of your success, don't wait for the storm to go r Caption

but start to learn how to dance in the rain, everyone will complain everyone will cry for their loss and their memory but you should not, focus on how to start and which step in next))
Chapter summary

i. Everything in life come when you have a true goal that you love and ready to sacrifice for
v. Build a true master inside your mind and work to make the world around better
v. Give your self-time and energy to achieve your goal in life

Always believe in your happens side of you, you must imagine you self-eying your life a havening, if you don't believe in yourself then who else is going to, draw your bright future with your brilliant magical hand and trust that you will one day become the hero of your own story the hero of your future , you are the core of the universe , the start of you galaxy and the light of the victory .

Make your time worthy

Make your people proud

Don't fear to jumbo into the battle

Rise like hero and speak like a man

You have only one life to live so what are you fearful of , make the most out of your day and night .

As the tow friend were sitting in the room the man said well it is time to reach to the city of Rome and get some self a tour in the allies of this mazing old city , because you all know we have in the Rome on the seven wonder of the worlds

Magical surrounding

The clock hits 8 AM and the three were still at the balcony after there was a blooming moments of prayers and meditation, and the sun raised above the eyes, the green scenery around has deplored and created a beauty green picture , the sky turned into blue colors combined with the sun light and white vacuum , it was absolutely splinter scenery.

I am happy that we were able to start our day like that it is just a magnificent. times that were invested that man has said, as we are here sitting in the balcony looking at this amazing view and this amazing garden that has been planted and destined by the old Rome people, the families that have lived here they turned their skills and masteries into a beautiful piece of art that really stood for us on how to use your abilities, skills , devotions to make your life worth to live and share it with other .

I want you all to remember the road and the journey that we all have been and never forget about every moments that you have spent here , life is about the journey and not about the end line .

That is so true Udayeh said , guess will always remember this bless hours that has come to us and how managed to enjoyed and manifested into a great life time .

The man said I want you to be more conscious about what you should do every morning and bring discipline to your life , and push yourself beyond your limits , so you can discover you ups and your flaws , don't be afraid to take a risk in your life , there is nothing to lose , don't wait for the right moment , but rather you make you right moment , as we have said you don't get to choose you future , but rather you choose your daily habits and your habits will choose your future , so check your habits very careful and try to changes to a better habits

Yes that for adding that Alan said , I think we are all drawn in our bad habits , we are so brains in given excuse to our bad habits to an existence that we believed our own lies , it time to really stand up and raise against our self

Choose a magical place for your mastery secret devoted future and dream plan and keep coming to it , daily to work in your goals and make this place very special to you , choose it side and open to get fresh air and sun light , everyday make a two how to come to this place and excite your plans steps , you need to choose this place with some feature such as a quiets one that you can think and work calmly , so you don't get distracted by outside , second this please should be open with fresh air coming in and coming out , all of the legend and master over the history use to stay in such places where they would be away from the outside noise and fantasy , and separated from the world , such as Steve job , Elbert enstain , Leonardo davinci and Bruce lei , Mohammad Ali , those people have a bites to stay alone and think for them self , working training and inventing artist and practices that they repeat over and over and over again and again until they master their work .

All science and studies should that you need to spend at least two hours alone doing your work until they master it , and later on they introduce their craft and art to the world so they can be a seen to all human kind , my advice to you is to find such place where you can do your work and plan at the highest maximum efficiency possible and make your self-devoted to what you do , so you can generate the best brilliant thoughts and ideas that will flow to you when you are searching . I remember once my old Master told me once that all ideas and legendry thoughts flow to you and find you , and you don't have to find it , it will find you and flow to you , when you set and do nothing but be at your best state of mind doing what you love , then the magic will happen and. You will sense signs and signal. You need your own space and environment that allows to be creative and high performance , the place that will push you to be inspired and aspire in this world , it is really important to have your own area that describe the Bryant and amazing part of you that want to be special and unique .

The averment you spend time on and you live in has trumeau's effects on you, and you job is to be able to make it work for you.
There are three elements you should pay highly attentions once you decide to execute on you plan there are these aspects to take care of.

- **First. your friends you spend the most time with:** people you spend have a huge impact and effects on your life and your standards, most of your belief and standards you grasped and soaked for people around that you spend time with such as you friends , family and partner .,

- The place you spend the time in : **the place you stay in has massive impact on your quality of your work and how efficient you are , the place can describe your value , dream ,thought and your standard , this place could be your table , your room and you apartment**

- **Your believe : the belief you have about your self have the most effects on you , this belief that you have formulate and create at the younger ages of your life from your family friends , others ... all of this is just a useless space inside need to be checked erased .**

Always try to make what is around you sparks your fire for your dream and light the genius part of you , and makes you feel that you are painting your life with manic and greatness , choose your people around wisely , choose human being who can inspire your and aspire you to be like the greatest person that you could be
I Hope you all enjoyed here because we are going on a short inspiring trip throughout the time and history the man has said.
we shall go and visited the old **colosseum** which is considered one of the seven wonders of the world along with **Tag Mahal** and **the Pyramid**, this Italian piece of art that has been hundreds of years ago and still tell now standing as one of the miracles of the world .
we need to move by 10 a.m. , after the coffee all of the three went down to move to the next place in Rome , they went down on the street , and one taxi stopped to pick them all , it was old Italian taxi driver , he was very kind with a big smile on his face he draw to them ,after he spoke in his Italian language , ciao , where are you going and finished with a kind words , I happy to serve .

the taxi car with all of the three men were moving inside the old city of Rome and the beauty of the city started to avail from the window of the car with every street they enter. the old architectures building of the city of Rome and the people walking around such a magnificent city the Man has said : have lived here for long time and it is still one of my favorite city in the world I love it is old tough that bring you back to time of Leonardo and the other legendry people , here is the home of the beautiful Italian opera and the magic symphony .

it is a such breath-taking place that I have devoted to visit and stay here since I was young it is really a creative land here in Rome .

(Don't think of the past, make the moment worth it , time is your only investment that you need to investee in daily , every Soule need to flourish and shine by it is creativity and it is genus that is hidden inside it , one need no accumulate negative thoughts but rather think wise and positive and move on with new day and new plane as the sun rise)

Once they reached the place from far the colosseum of the Rome started to appear with it is huge circle walls topped by the blue sky above it was such a magical view from far, everyone were excited and happy to be there.

What that is really incurable look to the old colosseum from far I could never be happier to see that, how could some build that it is so beautiful it must be a work of art , hand that is so skillful and charming , he brought this beautiful piece of increase art to the humanity , no wonder it is one of the seven wonders of the words ..

I totally agree Alan said , one just should set and enjoy this pleasing architecture , my eyes cannot believe what they are saying , I love this place I have always been in love with old places and old crafts since I was Young and now I am standing In front of this miracle of the human being , I guess this has be a work of art that has been inspired by god , it is really amazing , thanks sir for suggesting us to visit this place , it is really one of the most fascinating .... I have ever visit in my entire life , in think we are just surrounded full art and mastery here are no we ?

I guess we are Udayeh said . there must be a god guided and inspired hand behind this piece of mastery.

Let's all walk around this place it will be nice to sense the old history and the marks behind it . this colosseum which many also called it the Flavian amphitheater a big giant amphitheater built in the city of Rome started between 70 and 72 ce at the days of vespasin , next to the palatine Hill , on the ground of what was Nero gold house they said .

The artificial lake that was the centerpiece of that palace complex was drained , and they centered and sited the colosseum there , this choice was symbolic not just practical Vespasian.

The designing of the colosseum is so complicated itself and the structure was officially dedicated in 8- ce titus in a ceremony that included 100 days of games , and they have completed the work of the colosseum later by adding the uppermost story, unlike before .

Colosseum is a freestanding structure of stone and concrete, using a complex system of barrel vaults and groin vaults.

There be so Many details capturing this mazing place the artist behind took his time before he was able to manifest such art in his time .

Before we dive into the history of this mazing building lets me just speak to you about the rule of life that gives them .

There is the rule of 1% better, and this rule you can apply to all of the your life plan and task, if you ever want to achieve and reach a certain type of goal in your life , and it is a very complex one ,then you should apply this rule in your life and you will be able to break the task easily .

The rule state that if you want to reach a task that is very big and complex then all what you need is to get better one percent every week not every day and you will be able to reach , here is the catch my friends many of people just look at the last steps of the road , instead of just doing one small steps with a consistently and persistently to be better about one thing every day , and over the course of one3 year to decades you will master this technique and get a significant progress

And the one percent role goes like that :

1% progress

and

daily Actions

and

persistence

and

time

and results is success

And in order to unlock this process you need to do this technique so you can make though the actions.

be because you know that the rule says that:

consistency

is what

transform
average
into
excellence

○ Love what you do and enjoy the process, because as Steve jobs has said if you don't love what you do then you will not have the ability to keep going and have consistency and persistently

○ Keep doing it every single day unite it become a habit inside you, because the key to everything is to keep doing it every day as some descried that the process should be soaked inside and planter everyday within your heart so you

○ Give you self a treat or regards every time you make small progress so you can motive yourself, so keep pushing you self and keep you self motivat4d during the process and

○ Recheck your steps and progress and what you have achieve, always reach back and study your steps and progress so you can measure it and understand where you have reached to

○ Finally finish you mastery craft and enjoy being a experts in that thing and let the world see what you have achieve it

I guess the roman who built the comoluessn had the same thing they were as much as consistent and persisting with their work , I am supposed the engineer who were behind this piece of art had the love and the passion for their job , that why they were able to push it to the limit ,

The Colosseum (/ˌkɒləˈsiːəm/KOL-ə-SEE-əm; Italian: **Colosseo**[koloˈsːɛːo]) **is an oval amphitheatre in the centre of the city of Rome, Italy, just east of the Roman Forum. It is the largest ancient amphitheatre ever built, and is still the largest standing amphitheatre in the world today, despite its age. Construction began under the emperor Vespasian (r. 69–79 AD) in 72[1] and was completed in 80 AD under his successor and heir, Titus (r. 79–81).[2] Further modifications were made during the reign of Domitian (r. 81–96).[3] The three emperors that were patrons of the work are known as the Flavian dynasty, and the**

amphitheatre was named the Flavian Amphitheatre (Latin: *Amphitheatrum Flavium*; Italian: *Anfiteatro Flavio*[aɱfiteˈaː tro ˈflaː vjo]) by later classicists and archaeologists for its association with their family name *(Flavius)*.[citation needed]

\

The Colosseum is built of travertine limestone, tuff (volcanic rock), and brick-faced concrete. The Colosseum could hold an estimated 50,000 to 80,000 spectators at various points in its history[4][5] having an average audience of some 65,000;[6] it was used for gladiatorial contests and public spectacles including animal hunts, executions, re-enactments of famous battles, and dramas based on Roman mythology, and briefly mock sea battles. The building ceased to be used for entertainment in the early medieval era. It was later reused for such purposes as housing, workshops, quarters for a religious order, a fortress, a quarry, and a Christian shrine.[citation needed]

This remarkable architecture give the sign that there is a talent and mastery hidden inside each one of us, and that we should look for the thing in life that represent us and craft the Jim inside each one of us . before continue speaking about the colosseum I want to introduce steps to become a better version of yourself. if you want to growth and create a shift in your life then listen to these sequences of steps for you to apply in your life and premise me to apply in your daily routine and add it to your life.

Follow this goodness in your daily morning routine , wake up yourself early morning do yourself a calm meditation set your vision for the day and do some body movement excursive such as walking riming , push up and squads , after you finish this give yourself a cold shower to recover your energy , grab you self a coffee and start your 3 hours focused work on your life time goal after having a good healthy meal with less amounts of carbohydrates , at evening recheck your schedule if any remaining task di it.

Before you head to sleep do some short meditation to break you self from the day stress and overthinking , reflect on tomorrow and create vocation for you have a greater tomorrow to motivate your future state .and go to bed early to get what you need of rest

term e are many benefits for cold shower. Many scientist have spoken about the benefit of cold ice water after exercise in the morning , a studies have shown that cold ice water path in the morning can do miracles to the human body is good for increase you focus and make your mind clear of

any other negatives and flow thoughts that might distract your mind ,
which will make you feel relax and settled in .

one more benefit of the cold water shower is that it calm your anxiety
and recued your stress since it help your brain to focus on the drawing
signal coming from your body, because cold water increase your
circulation, since your first reaction to a polar ice blast of H2O is to move
away from it , cold water strain your body , the nature response to icy water
hitting your skin which is the key point here ,is that your system switch on
to survival mode .

the amazing thing here is that the shock that hit your body puts your
circularity system into overdrive and because of that your body increase
your blood flow to warm up your code and protect your vital organs and at
the same time it constricts your circulation near skin.

so the idea is to push yourself early in the morning and move your body
with excretive

Here is the redrawn of the success formula for you to follow and keep in
your mind

wake up 4:30

mediation + payers +success vision imagination

exercise + cold shower

+ two hours' work plan

reflect check on task

night mediation + morning vision

That is true life shifting program I want you all to have and be part of
your daily life, every person needs to put himself into displacing part so he
unlocks the unlimited potent ion inside him and release his superpower to
the action.

Yes, is truly mind shifting and life changing Udayeh said, I guess it is up
to us to learn the process and start working for our own life, really need to
check my old routine it has been giving me a stress and anxiety whenever I
try to do every morning, I used to always find myself busy and not
completing any task or work I do so many times and I have no well power
to complete, I guess we are all trapped in the same trap .

You are right Allan said I really need follow this process it feel like it
going to help me a lot in my life , I used to follow some process that I have
believed that it was the right one but none of that worked right for me , I
guess it is just not what I have wanted , remerge done time I tried to follow
some guru on TV and it was all not so well , I really need to know the right

steps for me to accomplish what I want in life, for the first time in my life I feel that I have changed to the right directions , and I have faced my struggles and myself ego ,

Yes that is nice the man said , I am really happy for you know I feel that we are getting the results from this journey all together , focused again on the craft that has been stamina here for hundreds of years and impressing the eyes of millions around the world .

The engine who has built this beauty stones has to be really proud of himself , he had no technology and modern tools and yet he able to come up with this amazing colosseum to our world .

start your peice of art

The construction was funded by the opulent spoils taken from the Jewish temple after the first Jewish roman war which lead to the siege of Jerusalem. according to a reconstructed inspiration found at that place in the site in Rome.

The emperor Vespasian has ordered this new amphitheater to be erected from general share of the booty. It is often has been though that the Jewish prisoners of war were brought back to Rome and contributed to the massive word force needed for the construction of the amphitheater , but there is no ancient evidence that can confirm that , it would be nonetheless with this free source of labor , teams of professional Roman builders

,engineers ,artist ,colosseum , the contractions of the colosseum has been done using different kind of materials such a s wood ,limestone , tuff ,tiles ,cement and mortar.

The designee of the colosseum has be darn before in a very unique way and were executed excellently , this Rome sightseeing has brought the interest and attraction to the archeology and historic, engine from all over around the world and it is very amazing how could this building stand , despite that the I liked **Taj Mahal** more , instill think that this colosseum is one of my favorite architected in the world , the empire who has built this Colloseum has defiantly wanted to present an authentic Italian art to the world filled with mastery and skillfulness mixed with history and old Italian .

It comes to us now to learn how the process to instructing such mesmerizing peace of art and how learn to make it last for over, we could think of all the greatest people throughout the history and just sense their genies and mastery in doing their work from Einstein ,Beethoven ,Mozart , Federer , Steve job and OTHERS ....

I have this old silver rings form the old Italian friend has given it to me, it is a valued piece of sliver please I need you to just take and keep it with you, while you do any kind of work and art just get inspired it and remember the piece of colosseum, I wanted to give you so you don't think that after you leave this place it is over here.

Thanks so much of that kind of you Udayeh said, this stone on the top surface has the symbol Rome empire with the green around him, it is really great gift .

Alan oh that a lot we are really fascinating about being here and learning the greatest art and wisdom that has travelled through the history, I already feel that I belong to this place despite that I have just came here few days ago, this place really got into me and make feel the piece and joyful from the inside.

((Remember it is always you who shake your world, it is you who move the mountain of sorrow to jump into the hills of legendry and mastery, learn to smash your fair with massive actions, learn to build your own magical world inside your, that no one can break into it, you have the power to spread your magic around the world))

Udayeh: Everything in life created for a reason and you are the center of this universe, your eyes shine of dreams and success, it noticeable when you rest in peace and think of nothing sitting around in your area looking at the start and the blue sky , looking at the greater colosseum for side , it is just a peace where you can truly see the really you that is hidden or has been hiding for a long time .

One day we will wake up and say we wish we had the chance to fight for what we wanted and had in our hand, but life will give so many chances and turn in and turn our we will ignite out world with pure love and passion toward what we do and what we give.

Let's give our self the chance to shine and sink into the path of success and legendry.

For every emotions you receive from someone it is role to make you stronger and more wiser for the upcoming stages in your life for every sorrow, sadness, rages and happiness it meant to come to your life to create a new pattern to be more joyful and strength in your life, so learn every emotion what is the reason behind it , how to deal with it , until you master yourself and your body .

That is so true my friend Udayeh, nice to see you understanding life as it is , no more than a journey for us to live and experience ,we shall experience everything from happiness to darkness , but at the end a paint of our journey will be drawn , there is so much power and greatness inside each one of us ,it is for us to disclosed, if you build the right the habits as we have spoken before you shall build a life filled with joy and happiness that will spread all over to your kid and you families that will come after you , there is a great advice for you on how to become more focused and more calm , the key here is to teach yourself to control you emotions and your reactions , because evet9ng actions will have a reactions , you know not so many people knows how to control their emotions , they can get angry very fest and lose their temper , which a very dangerous act , some will say he is just expressing his feeling and will relax after , and that is absolutes not true , my. Greater teacher : **SAID**

((you should never give someone the privilege to make your angry or happy their kind of thing you have to keep it for yourself)).

Your emotions usually come from your motions, and whatever you focus on the energy will flow into so keep yourself calm and teach yourself focused on the right thing sand good thing that are.

Every emotion as it have been known comes my friends from your information and data that you collect from your five senses such as eyes image ,ears sounds ,noise smell ,hand touch feeling ,so your brain works on receiving this data and make it in format of memory all together and your emotions is how your react to this information all together , it is better to learn how to control your emotions and how you can master you self-control of your body and mind .

Every step of success and failure will be filled with a lots of memory and emotions then you will sink into your mind learn how to understand your emotions and your mind together learn how to become calm and less reactive , become receiver to reactor toward your stuffy

So you emotions sources are:

Memory

Image

Sound

smells

((Your life is a reflection of your thoughts and emotions about past, present and future and you can choose how to make your life to be like, when you change your perception towards everything))

SEVEN

LIFE AUDIT

Coming back the history of the colosseum at the old time of Romanian Era where the building of the Colosseum began under the rule of Vespasian where the third of the colosseum had been completed at that time, the top level of the construction have been completed at the time of his son.

The colosseum was used in the old times as a church, after that it was used as a fortress by some families, the name of the colosseum was chosen because of it is huge size and massive space of area that is taking, beside to the colosseum building there was a statue for the emperor Nero which give it another reason why it is called like that.

This history in Rome has been an attraction to many visitors around the world, and many has been visiting it every day, you can still feel the history when you are walking around it, there used to be a battle among wild animals from different place of the world vs some prisoners who use to be slave people, which was very famous around the world during the time of Romanian emperors.

Let me just move to the life you want to make and create with yourself, there are a great deal within your when you want to build your life that you want to achieve in the future, you have to start from now so you can build the track or the line that you need to follow , give you self-time to start writing your life audit for your goals and dedicated yourself to the things that mean a lot for you .

If you want to really make a courage step to ignite the spark of genius inside and release the beast inside you, launch the power that is hidden within, then you need really to know the right monologue of manifesto for you, the correct formula for you to act upon on , you need to know also as I have said before what where when and why you are doing what you are doing .

Make what you want close to your heart and coming from inside your soul and body, let me help my dear friends by introduce the right manifesto for you to be able to make that happen, let me just offer my humble method to you to start living a life that you really want .

Before you start to live your life and fight for your dream you need to know how to fire your life with more charm and

Financially

Career:

Relationship

Spiritually

As for you to really start building your ultimate life you should draw the lines that you will start attract

Life audit

1-Plan your 8 areas of your life

If you want to start to build your greater life and chase your dream you need to work on the parts of your life , which are important , it is very essential to work on this areas of your life which are

Health: if you want to build a stronger life that filled off with joy and fulfillment you should never neglect your health part of your life, and that could be your mental health not just your body healthy, to be take care and will spending you time on enhancing this aspect of your life , how can you enjoy your success and your life without having the perfect body and the perfect mind ,

So, you have to work on tow element of your health

1- your body: your shape, your fitness, your ability to work and walk

2-Your mind: your mindset, your thought, your ability to control your ideas and thoughts , because you know my dear friend that is very important

Growth: if you want to upgrade your life quality and get a better level of sense and joyful within you, you must really take some consideration to upgrade your personal growth, your communications skills and your daily aspect of your life must be upgraded by you .

In today's world, you don't need to go to college or university to acquire a skill. You can learn from someone who has done it and is sharing it on the internet.

There are plenty of courses are offered online and people are getting more and more conscious about learning and improving themselves.

If you don't commit to learning and improving regularly, you will be soon become obsolete. You will be out of business. Your junior will overtake you in your job and when the tough time comes, your company will have to let you go because you are dispensable.

And the only way to make sure you are indispensable is to constantly upgrade yourself.

Just yesterday, I bought an online course about real estate investment. I read about 2 to 3 books every month and I make sure I attend a workshop or seminar at least once a year.

Relationships: one of the key factors that you should pay attentions two is your relationship around , your relations with you family , friends and life partner should you be attentions closely to the type of relationship that you have in your life it is very important to have people in your life that pushes forward and feed you with love and support that you need , this area of your life is very important and it will affect your life a lot if it is not well and healthy , for you to launch the ideas and genius track path that you need every time your relationship need to level up to the challenges , someone once said that your relationship from y

As the tow friend were sitting in the room the man said well it is time to reach to the city of Rome and get some self a tour in the allies of this mazing old city , because you all know we have in the Rome on the seven wonder of the worlds

Magical surrounding

The clock hits 8 AM and the three were still at the balcony after there was a blooming moments of prayers and meditation, and the sun raised above the eyes, the green scenery around has deplored and created a beauty green picture , the sky turned into blue colors combined with the sun light and white vacuum , it was absolutely splinter scenery.

I am happy that we were able to start our day like that it is just a magnificent. times that were invested that man has said, as we are here sitting in the balcony looking at this amazing view and this amazing garden that has been planted and destined by the old Rome people, the families that have lived here they turned their skills and masteries into a beautiful piece of art that really stood for us on how to use your abilities, skills , devotions to make your life worth to live and share it with other .

I want you all to remember the road and the journey that we all have been and never forget about every moments that you have spent here , life is about the journey and not about the end line .

That is so true Udayeh said , guess will always remember this bless hours that has come to us and how managed to enjoyed and manifested into a great life time .

The man said I want you to be more conscious about what you should do every morning and bring discipline to your life , and push yourself beyond your limits , so you can discover you ups and your flaws , don't be afraid to take a risk in your life , there is nothing to lose , don't wait for the right moment , but rather you make you right moment , as we have said you don't get to choose you future , but rather you choose your daily habits and your habits will choose your future , so check your habits very careful and try to changes to a better habits

Yes that for adding that Alan said , I think we are all drawn in our bad habits , we are so brains in given excuse to our bad habits to an existence that we believed our own lies , it time to really stand up and raise against our self

our friends ,wife family are a reflection of your standard , so take a look to the kind of relationship that you have try to analyze and ,

When you're deeply in love with someone, you feel happy and good. You perform better and deliver greater jobs.

Conversely, when you are not doing well in your relationship, other areas of your life may suffer. You can't concentrate on your work because all you think about is why someone you love has dumped you.

Each relationship in your life is unique and, with that, each relationship may serve a slightly different purpose in your life. For example, a romantic relationship may teach you what you value in a partner. A close sibling relationship may teach you the meaning of unconditional love and companionship.

Every relationship has its own purpose and value, but, as a whole, there are ways for you to improve relationships in order to better your life as a whole. We will get into those specific goals later.

Career: you should know what kind of area in life you are good at and that you truly enjoy doing, your career is very important for you so try to make this area of your life very successful and not stressful to you, you career will take large amount of your life , so you should focus on getting the right career that gives the right return ,

2- mind set shift: sometime all what you need is a shift your mind set so that you can see everything differently so if you ever got stuck in your mind and never were able to move ahead or get things right then you

better thing really shift your mind set, your standard are low your life are not up to the challenges , and the mindset Factor is so big in such a way that sometime you win before you even do you move you activate you plan on the ground , and that is how strong the Mind shift side of you , it is to that extent the mind can affect you and your life you need to be more careful on how you could become a better thinker , on how to upgrade your own level of Mind sometimes it is not easy to do this shift , it takes days , months and sometimes years , and you think that people will always support you when it is not the case , you own life can be only determine by how you react but also how you act while you do your own life style

3- create a vision:try to look away and draw a future plan for what you want to be in the future, your brain has an amazing power to just create a visualization and manifest what it want , when create an image for what you want in the future then your brains and mind will automatically guide and take for what you want to be ,

Don't expect a clear and well-defined vision overnight—imagining your life and deciding on a course of action takes time and reflection. You must cultivate vision and perspective, as well as apply logic and planning to put your vision into action. Your best vision emerges from your hopes, dreams, and aspirations. It will resonate with your values and ideals, generating energy and enthusiasm to help strengthen your commitment to exploring your life's possibilities. The question appears to be simple, but it is frequently the most difficult to answer. Allowing yourself to explore your most primal desires can be terrifying. You may also believe you don't have time to think about something as fanciful as what you want out of life, but it's important to remember that a fulfilled life is not usually the result of chance, but of design.

Asking thought-provoking questions can help you discover the possibilities of what you want out of life. Consider every aspect of your life, personal and professional, tangible and intangible. Contemplate all the important areas, family and friends, career and success, health and quality of life, spiritual connection and personal growth, and don't forget about fun and enjoyment.

4 - daily work and consistency:

Once you found you self the right vision and the goal that you are wishing to get to, it is then when you should know that the only thing that will get you to that certain goal is the consistency and the continuing of the working on a daily basis , because every art and every craft needed a spark and a light to make it work .

As I have mention to you before on this elements of consistency and persistent it is the hero and the legend people character , they never stop working for their dream and their life that they want to achieve , wither it is raining m sunny ,cloudy , or desert you should choose your path , you should never give up on your goal , give your work and your goals the magic of consistency and check what is going to happen on your life , give your work the MAJIC OF persistency and keep pouching up until you know and feel that you have given all what you can do then it is then when your results start to disclose and happen for you .

Only miracles and heaven will happen with consistency and persistency , but the question is what are the things that help you to be consistent and persisting in your work ,job ,plan and all of other things in your life , the answer is here there are many things that are very important for you to be able to fight and be persistent in your work of your craft and this things are the follow :

You should love what you do and be passion about, because otherwise how you think that you are going to keep fighting and not being bored or stressed when you do such thing in your life , the only thing that will push you forward and make more persistent and subtle for your goal is that idea that you love what you are doing in your life , how to know that you are doing what you love , well here how :

1 you enjoy when you do it and you feel happy .

2 You feel so fulfill from the inside when you do it and you become abundance from the other world outside.

3 You never get bored of doing every day and you wake in the next morning excited to work again and doing over and over .

4- you keep thinking of it no matter how much you get busy in your life and it is like that it become part of your life .

That is so true Udayeh said , I really sometime enjoy playing piano and tennis , and once I do that I completely feel happy and joyful from the inside and for that I think this really true what you have said , there were so many time in my life when I felt confuse and not sure of what I am dong in my life , you need to be able to focus on your goal , you need to focus on the thing that matters to you, do not attract what you don't wont , just keep yourself busy with the thing that give you strings and motive to keep going , change your friends you place but keep you self-growing and changing .

5 – purpose or mission: for you to become really series and passionate about your work , you should set a purpose and the mission that is set behind the goal , every goal should be concerned with mission that give it is meaning , a mission can make your goal more deep align it with your life , make your goal worldwide and it is better to choose a goal that affect the world , your business can be set upon that goal .

Once you have that goal and purpose in your life it is will make it easy for to follow up with your work

7-Enjoy the process:during doing your work as we have said , if you are enjoying your work and filling shake from the inside , then it means that you love you work and you are then going to enjoy your life and your goal, you cannot keep thinking about the future and do not live the present , the present was future at some point , so why don't you live for a while and keep in your heart what you want to achieve or do in life .

You should be able to love yourself and love the journey that you have been going in do not think that life is a matter of taking and earning , by that kind of mind set you will lose yourself and become flat sided person .

Be wise enough to live in every moment you have in your life , time is the most priceless thing you will ever have in your life beside family , so time with family is so valuable it gives you motive and hope for you keep going on with your on journey in life , take every chance you get in your life to enjoy and smile , help other , what is the worth of this life if your made only about the material and what you have gained and earned from work and people , but the real thought is that life is what you have left in people heart , and what you have done to become more of a better person .

You take a look and see how your circle of life could look like if you were able to well organized it:

Just getting back to the colosseum and it is beautiful construction , it have been so years passed during the time of building the colosseum , this place is just a reminder for you my two friends how your life can be so could and amazing once your turn on the greatness and genus inside , and you open the door for the magic to surround your work and your life ,

The ancient roman people have given a lot of time to their armies power to get significant and keep the vast empire , and keep this empire under control , the roman has place a high importance in the acritude of it cities , this architecture played a significant role in the maintaining control of the roman empire by creating constant ,visible symbol of their world. The roman have used their building to advance in their knowledge of the colosseum .and now in this time of our present day the colosseum represents the major points of roman society, militaristic architecture nature and elegant architecture

This make the site of the colosseum so attractive to the whole Rome city and the surrounded places and many of the world places , this made it a very significant to it is position , many have considered this construction the main symbol of Rome greatness and it is deep massive history and position in the eunoto and world civilisations .

That is decently not to be argued against Alan said , I have felt so many writer describing the place and importance if this majesty building I think sometimes you just need to set and look around you without speaking any words , because you're feeling and your imagination should speak up first before your mouths, your sense of Mastery should be ignited from the inside out , having a great people around and doing what we do is just a great honor for me , I had a great words of wisdom and advice from you.

Even in the old books and tells this mesmerizing building has took place, just by looking at it from far distance you can just feel the history run inside of you, and your blood pump up with the old civilization, I guess we are all here happy and satisfied to fill out eyes with this huge mark in the history of the Europe and the world.

I used to think I am just going to see this building in the to and magazine only Udayeh said , the power of human be can be just unlimited if you were able to just unlock the keys within you and launch your passion and love while you are chasing your dream.

There are many time in my childhood were I thought that there is limit for myself and for my abilities , and I felt that I am restricted with the barriers around , the barriers form the future and from the past ,with the present , I have kept this believe for a long time since , I have based on this beehive kept myself from doing anything or challenging myself but I was lucky to travel to India and then to Italy , that was so blessed for me to happened because you never know were the world could take you so your open your talent and your power .

ALAN I took so many challenges my life , I was able to learn to hit tennis and play some music , this give me some magical area in my life and left me joyful and abundance in some time , I started to love to talk to people and listen to their opinion as a r4espect to them .

I am standing in front of this huge building and feeling just joyful and excited about the future and about my life that how amazing it is going to be

The Man said :

The colosseum was built in a time after a significant political shift . the Romans were moving on from the line of emperors after Caesar as the roman empire was reaching its peak ,they wanted to show their superiority through architectural marvels like the colosseum , initially the building was built to mark the reign of Vespasian an emperor who took power after the disastrous rule of Nero. It showed stability in a time of political unrest .there was an almost militaristic order to the exterior with it evenly spaced arches and the

Interior with tis structural circulation . the very structure itself had a constant rhythm of arches around the façade. It also solidified the change of power from Nero to Vespasian.

The building performs "political manipulation" by removing Nero's mark on Rome.

The structure was massive gift to be used by the citizen of Rome.

((Wake up to the life , look up and see you are very colourful and beautiful from the inside out, you are kind to win , you are powerful to show and you are genus to live without fear of failure))

Chapter summary

There are many things to remember in life and that one can get through in , last remember this always :

- Have a purpose in life that keep you awake and motivated , it is better to make broad wide one .

- Enjoy the journey of your own while trying to achieve more in live that is one to remember don't deprive yourself from having fun in excuse of work and duty , don't kill your own life .

- Build a warm environment around , from friends family , works filled with love , respect and gratitude .

- Create a healthy mind that can support during the journey , and that is so important and crucial to greatness and Mastery .

EIGHT

RULE FOR GREAT LIFE OF THE MOST EFFECTIVE BILLIONAIRES AND PEOPLE LIFE CHANGING

Thad man contained his talk about the colosseum , when the colosseum was first opened in the past , at that time the emperor ha celebrated with the very known famous 100 days of games of gladiatorial, where it was very familiar around the world , even the emperor has performed in the arena many time.

Many re-enactments and public execution have been hosted in the arena also , The floor of the colosseum, where you might expect to see a smooth ellipse of sand, is instead a bewildering array of masonry walls shaped in concentric rings, whorls and chambers, like a huge thumbprint. The confusion is compounded as you descend a long stairway at the eastern end of the stadium and enter ruins that were hidden beneath a wooden floor during the nearly five centuries the arena was in use, beginning with its inauguration in A.D. 80. Weeds grow waist-high between flagstones; caper and fig trees sprout from dank walls, which are a patchwork of travertine slabs, tufa blocks and brickwork. The walls and the floor bear numerous slots, grooves and abrasions, obviously made with great care, but for purposes that you can only guess.

The guesswork ends when you meet Heinz-Jürgen Best of the German Archaeological Institute in Rome, the leading authority on the hypogeum, the extraordinary, long-neglected ruins beneath the Colosseum floor. Best has spent much of the past 14 years deciphering the hypogeum—from the Greek word for "underground"—and this past September I stood with him in the heart of the great labyrinth.

This talk about the amazing and the beauty of the colloeseum could just go on and on to an never end , the stories behind it and the life that has been brought to us by exampling and wandering around this great place .

I just want to be honest with you , did not expect for me to be happy a lot with this tour and spirit visit to this mesmerizing place , you have come close my heart and I truly mean it .

Udayeh: I thank you too I had never thought that such place would bright my eyes and light my heart , it has open so much inside of me today and for the future to come it is really great pleasure to have this chance to witness and wander at this historical symbol of skills and greatness ,w ill be remember this visit for the rest of my life I thanks you so much from the button of my heart sir with much hope to catch with such amazing chances in the future days .

I guess i had this on my backlist Alan said , it was a great experience and test for our mind and soul to do this visit and feel the history comes to life again , of course this is going to last for ever with me , there has been so much awaking within me with every step. We have made at this visit I guess we are so lucky and bless just to come here and fill our eyes with this piece of art and craft that has become a symbol for greatness and mastery that has lasted tell the day of today .

I much thanks to you both the man said , and let me just tell that it is much amazing to get to such wisdom and genius inside just by looking deep incised and awake the artist that indie your heart .

There are so much hidden for you both in the future so please take a chance and invest in your talent and invest in what love and your advocate , once youth start your really journey because you know what you need is that something that set you and take you to the greatest level of master and bring the best artist that is within you , because if you do something that you truly love and your passion about then it will last for every , and you will never be bored or given up on .

((Stupid people do things they don't like because they think it is their duty , smart people they do things they love and they enjoy to some extinct. , but genius people do thing they need to do only and they enjoy their whole life))

A man once said , if you said along in silence and did nothing , what you love and what you need will flow to you naturally without any effort

look deep insdie of your always

From Taj mahal , to the Hanging Garden of Babylon to to . , to . , to All of this place and marvels just tell that there is no limits indeed each one of you , and you are able to reach the greatness and Master that is within you ,every day you spend Is a step for you to build that ,every decision your make should be helping you to get closer to what you want . Remember to meditate every day because it clear your mind and make you more focused and award of what you are doing , overthinking could damage your state of your mind and make you do unrations actions without planning

There are four sides will benefits you when you practice meditation :

1. **Understanding your pain** : once you start mediation and your mind starts to shift into the state of theta or and relaxing mode , you will start to identify what you really need or what you are suffering from. Because your mind will transfer to it is ultimate state that possible which is the stare of focus and energy accumulation in one place of the time and place ,and at that points you will be able to feel your pain

1. **Lower your stress** : one of the main key and be nights to mediate is to put you in state of relaxation and lowering your overthinking energy sucking problem ,

3. **Connect better** :

once you be able to focus more and control your thus and your ideas together , after you have reduce you stress and you nastier , then will help connecting better with yourself and with your surroundings , and especially your friends and your love once to the level of joy and full connecting abundance , Trust my friends never cut a small wondering in the sky in the morning with light sun light this will make so much power ,because how you start you day is how you end it , once you are truly awake in the moment and every part of your body is alive , once very breath you take is depend you are feeling it , once you thought are clear and flowing naturally you will be in your idle state to receive and communicate with the world flowing .

4- Be Present in :doing mediating will help to live the current moment of time not the past and not the future , since your thoughts are most of the time are resourced from the past and the future being in state of meditating and flowing easily , mediation will train your brain and yourself to become award at the present not the past nor the future , even for me there is no sign day passes by without doing a set of short time mediation so I can clear my mind and become more focused and solid for the day .

5-Shifting energy toward your side

this is very important to know beside when you are not present, and your mind is shatters that means that your focus is shifted everywhere and your energy is going everyway wasted but not to you , having a meditation practice makes your thoughts once and your focus in place , which will shafts your energy on the right direction at the present moments

6. **-Reduce brain chatter**

: because of the nature of your brain , it keeps working and thinning even when you are sleep you brain keeps functions and analysing your data that you have received from the your day light , for that your brain most of time is busy with thoughts and emotions

((Set in quit place alone and try to notice your trend of thought and your line of energy , think of what you love and what you have done for the last week , you will feel that you Soule and your mind will become more active , helping feeling more alive and abundance from the inside))

Udayeh: I really enjoyed this spread of wisdom that you have brought to us, that was really enlighten to us

I think we are all blessed just to have the ability to think and decide for our self and choose our future and for that we need to keep searching and learning more about what need to do ,

I think sometime we get trapped in the loop of over thinking and not knowing what to do exactly so for that we need to just take break of everything and restore our peace and calm to our Soule and mind, there are millions of ideas and information floating in the world, we need to settle on the right one to use our time and energy in the right way .

Life is so short to not do what you love and what you hope for ,

Alan you are definitely right we are all in this positions together still trying to find our self in this messy world , where there are so many spaces around to discover , I guess that when it come to our mind and our soul where everything start form , I always have been dreaming of reaching to some points of my life where I don't have to worry about anything or care about anyone that stand in the way of my dreams and my passion to life , having a great practice of meditation can help anyone to reach such place in our life being ,

The man :That right my friends I hope that you are become in aware of yourself and what you are seeking in this life , because here is the key point unless you discover yourself and your potential , you cannot move to outside and flourish in the air , and unleash your superpower , there have been so many battles and discussion in the history of human being about the secret of wellbeing and what are the technique for the ancient Egypt civilization to the Greek era to the roman and the all of the other civilizations of the human being .

After all it is all simple juts start from where you are and what you have , look deep down inside of you , what are the things that accelerate the beats of your heart and makes your spirits fly in the galaxies , what are the rituals that you never bored of doing even in the toughs time of your life , what are the moments where you felt that the time has stopped and everything els does not matter at all .

((Times fly any way whether you smiled or you cried , time fly and passes whether you run or you walked or you crawled , time passes whether you succeed or you failed , but all come to what have you felt while this time ran out , what kind of energy you have given to the world and what kind of energy you have received from , so it is better to do what you love and what you think it is more represented of your Soule and you heart))

How to find what you really want and what you need to do in life ?
What is your loving art passion mastery ?
What is you motivational ?
What is your burning desire ?
How know what do you want in this life ?

The three keep moving in there walk around the colosseum and within their eyes there were the charm of the building and the place , with the green area that is surrounding the place the , and there were a small pool of water within statue in the middle , the sound of water were so deep , three of them sat on a edge of rock .

The man said I could just imaging how overwarming this place and setting looking to the colosseum from this side how much time and history has passed on this place .

I want you to keep doing your work on the most joyful way with so much passion ad love , ever care about could happen in the outside ad around , before you go to sleep just give you self a few time to write down :

What are the most joyful thing that made happy during the day .

What ate the thing that are negative ad you want to change it .

Any thoughts or good flow inside your mind that inspired during the day

.

((At the end of our journey I thought that I need to share with you such methods and ideas on how to know yourself and how to choose the right path for you , this is a very important idea that you need to suck it in your life))

This small tactics will help to make sure you are doing the things that you love in your live and based on that you can be more aware and focused o the things that you want the most and just keep smiling to everything that is around no matter how it feel bad inside , because you don't want that spark to get turned off inside of you .

Here my journey with me came to end , I was very happy or spend this amazing time with , and I hope one day you will be able to draw you dream and spark some on your way , please your life is your choke and your right so make sure you live the most of it in the most fulfilled way and give yourself what you need and what you want to growth and flourish .

Ask you self-everyday am I doing what I love and does what I love in front of me , or is it somewhere else so please don't mind other people who are small minded who try to talk you out of it .

;

Udayeh : That is a very amazing advice from you , you have really enlighten our road , we have could not been more happy that we are now , all of this time has passed here in Rome here and I could feel it

Alan : where are the most blessed and honoured to have you with us on this blessed tour ,

Remember you both to ALWAYS carry with the dream and passion , keep your eyes awake on what you see around ,every day is a chance for you to growth and to move one step closer to your dream ,build your rituals habits that will make successful and more ambitious that before , be grateful to what you have while seeking what you have I your life because you will ever own everything's I life, so why or try to be happy now and let go of every thoughts that is trying to take away from your moments .

I just want to say that I will miss so much and just until next journey or life trip keep doing and keep going forward with your life , carry on with all what you have had ever let and allow anyone to push back and turned you away from your dreams .

((Remember life is all about experience not just about awards and trophies that you hold or have so always become what you need and live every day to the foulest then always you will become unstoppable I your journey))

Both of the three wet back to the hotel room next to the famous garden in later cantered by an old phantom that has a statue of an old Romania solder in the middle , with water flowing in the air , the man then left to his place preparing to his flight to Iraq which he will visited some secret old place that only exhibit in books and magical stories .

Before he leave he gave the two friends a note book to read while on their way back to their place on the train.

((Life will through in fort of you so may obstacle ad walls that will make feel like you are weak but the true think here is that this is just a path for you to your dream and to you wonderful life and journey , by just keep moving and trying toward what you want you will know that every battle is just a greater lesson and way to transform into the best version of yourself))

Chapter 8

Rules of the Mastery for the greater Life

10 Tactics for you to become the best person you could be :

1-**Kindess** : it is a very small a pure advice for to ever miss a chance o being kind To someone, or a chance for you to give had to someone that you know or member of your family because you are here as a servant for humanity of all kind , smile at your worst cases or coition , be positive about the things that you could be in the future , learn to dance in the storm believe if you do that for often time with consistency you will train your brain to function that way , that how the mind set of genius and great one is all about .

Don't be greedy to be kind to someone or generate effort of love and compassionate you never when it is your turn to become the one who need that help , how many time you miss a chance to be kind or you have lost your emotion later or you had that kind of deep regrets inside that you were spoors to be the nice guy or light other people heart and support their dream with hope and sparks to keep going .

because you never know when the last moment for you on the planet will come.

i rather to smile at my worst moments , I'd rather to dance in the storm then to wait for the big party celebration to start laughing and dancing , I choose to be happy now then to wait for the big moments to come , my life start from now looking inside of me of how much creation that living with me , how much small cells and microbiology is helping me to survive every day , I should be thanking to keep moving away and smile every day to Eveready one who is near me just to convey the good energy to the people around me who might really needed to keep living .

1- keep your shoulder strait and your head up :

I always try to keep my shoulder up and my head or face strait up in air , once you conditions your face to be like that you will start training you mind that you are always confident and build that kind confident inside you ,

My second good tip you would be to keep your shoulder strait and your head up so your body align with your mind in the process of telling yourself that you are a fighter and nothing can stop you in your story , don't lean to the ground and never ever put your head down just because you have felt one day that you are unworthy of value, or because of someone has told so ,so please keep your head up and move ahead with a confided revalue to be more happy and successful , my greater friend Jordan Peterson says in his greater book ((12 rules for life)) one of his basic and important rule is to keep your shoulder up and standing so you believe physically , and that is very true because the science tell us today that many of our belief and our perspective about our self comes from out body posters and the way we move , your body will posture will tell you how your mind is thinking and telling about you value for yourself , and it is a greater advice .

Keep you vision up and very insincere and clear , keep you hope and your positivity energy up so you can get more blesses and awareness of the true joy and life time , don't waste your time being hard on yourself just because someone told you are not worthy of nothing , that is nothing relate of you truly are , because you are just reacting to what people are saying about you , you are just reacting to their thought and their words , your value comes from yourself and from the work that you dedicated for you self to growth in life and aspire a new way of thinning and understanding life , your value are the time you spend with your self-telling yourself that you are a greater person with a greater heart so don't you ever create your vale from other because you are 100% responsible for your own life , and the rest is just an illusion that flying around , just like the wind fly around the mountains it never moves it or shake it because the mountain are the solid fact the it weight is enough I tell that . be the mountain in the face of the life and keep your body active and energetic so you get to be more joyful successful in your life .

2- Stay Motivated : as I have said you before there is nothing more powerful than a greater work that is keep happening by one person , there is nothing more clear and heavy on the world that a plane that has been followed without time wasted , for you to get the results you need the compound effect results , you need to keep your shoulder up in the air and keep you plan in the actions , and active on the ground that is the secret for everyman and women to need their life to be shifted toward the better place , the arrow for it to be strong and accurate within while it hit its target need to be strait and in one line while it is moving .

So just keep working every day to make your goal real , for you to stay in the battle you need to keep showing for the world every day to prove that you are you are moving forward .

((The cycle for it is to stay balanced it need to stay moving ahead other side it will fall aside, the plan for it to stay flying it need to keep flying and moving up in the sky and it should not stop for any reason only in the case of landing , and so the same for human in life for them to stay alive they need to keep growing)

3- Serve and contribution :

If you want your work to become more blessed that has deep meaning and growth it is effect vastly , you need to make this work for other , you inside goal while making this goal should be dedication to provide serve and help to other in their life if you want have the ultimate return back on your work it must be a humanities goal with a mission to seek , before you start selling or creating or education you must make you goal clear , worldwide , pure , human life changing , providing a serving to the people , and most important your work must bring contributing to the world .

Then once you assured this things your work will transcend and become a greater work purely for the purpose of making the world better , every time you need to sell new product or painting a new pain , writing a new song , manufacturing some product give this kind of work a meaning , and ask yourself WHY …. Why I am doing … why it is important … who should get benefit from it …how I can make change outside by making the unique work .

Make you self-responsible before you choose to follow any kind of work or ideas , give you self the time to manufactured a genius gifted magical work and arts , give you self the space and place to work on your great idea and will bring change you and to the world , attract the right people to help to do so .

4- Rest , Reset ,Recheck :

IT IS a greater advice I would like to give to you , that will help make sure you are doing the right thing in your life , if you want to make sure that you are doing the right plan , if you want to assure that you are really started working on your goal , every time you need to take a rest a setback for a while , then give you self a time to check whether you work is matching the goal , reset you plan and your steps , then give it a general check , that how you can analyse and examined your work whether it is on the right track or not .

Every time you feel that there is something not working in your plan just give you self a break time to just rest yourself and body and your Soule it be able pure yourself from all the materials and fake goal and hint that has been accumulated inside your head , and to pure your goal and your mission form such thing that has been gathered in your progress , again you can also check the progress and the change that you have made whether it fetching with your real mission , many times you might get distracted by barriers around or ideas and opinions about your work , it is very important to make sure that your work is landing on the right page .

5-**BRING POSITIVE:**

It a always good to be prepare to transmit a positive energy to everyone around , from the first day you start your day keep promise to yourself that you will be a transitive machine to everyone , and you will always be kind when it is possible to , this will make you very blissful and joyful from the inside , and at the end of the day you will feel enormously happy and satisfy .

It does not matter what is going on in your life , remember that how did you react is the important thing , train yourself to always stay optimistic about anything , there is nothing good last for ever , and there is nothing bad also last for ever, so why not keep your temper on check and ask yourself why I am not smiling right now , what stop me from being positive and highly energetic t the moment.

Your friends and love one will need always nice words and support at their lowest moments in life , sometime your smile and words will mean a lots to them ,so remember always shine like sun and radiate a positive energy to everyone around , because one day this all will come back to you at many form of gestures .

We need to keep track of our behaviour during the day we should not allow anyone to control our self and how we feel this is always out choice and responsibility to manage our actions and reactions .

6- **Be an ACTOR Not a Reactor :**

this always a good advice a try to give to every clients of me , IN every EVENTS OR SITUATION IN YOUR LIVE JUST TRY TO BE an actor nor a reactor , and this is very important to know the different between this two concept .

Reactor : is the try to react to everyone or each situation that happened around you using deep emptiness whether it is sad or anger , the when you are reactor this will mean that you are always a slave to someone behaviour , you are always a mirror to everyone actions , so if you do you bad things you will immediately react badly and if they do you good thing it is just the same , in other world you are giving them the pleasure to control you mood and chasing you temper , you are down to any bad actions to change you self to the worst ,

But on the other hand ACTOR : is the one to start the actions and without being affected by other actions , in a another way when you are an ACTRO you are the source of your own actions and reactions , you are the source of your own feeling and decisions , but when you are a reactor then you are not the source of your actions but other people behaviour and actions are the source of your feeling , so why give the pleasure to anyone to control your Mood and your behaviour just drop any dean or opinion about you and start control your own behaviour to other .

Always remember that other people opinion is the their own imagine about you . it is what they have concluded about you , which is mean it is just a theory or just a reactions on you that they tried to make think that it is what you are , and here is small tips for you to stop being reactor and to be only an ACTOR :

- Never use devices or serf social media in the morning because it will make react to everything randomly
- Remember to thing before you talk or talk any kind of actions this will monitor your brain and your behaviour
- Always smile to relief stress from outside negative sources of energy

7-Everyting in your Mind :

whatever thoughts you had in your mind it has been generated in your mind only , all the Drama that you generated in your daily life has been created by your own mind affected by your emotions , feeling and memories , once your mind is being directed in the right way and you organised your thoughts then your life will much easier so do your efficiency and energy of your work will become higher and deeper .

any bad event or trouble you faces in your life your mind works on ....it and make it looks bigger and bigger , giving you all the worst possibilities that could happen in a smart way and evaluable 99% of this thoughts and negatives conclusion that has been created by the mind never happen , so the key is to look to the problem as it is never make worst , and think resonantly not emotionally .

there are 5 things can help you control your mind :

1-everily morning mediation .

2- reading books .

3-talking to positive friends about your struggles .

4-think of the better future and .

5- sleep well and play sport to get positive energy physically .

6-talk in a positive way and think positively because your thoughts and behaviour attract the same .

7- clean your environments around and breath a fresh air .

8-give hand of help to anyone that you could .

8-**build a legacy and heritage behind you** :

In your life while trying to reach to your top of your dream and doing a nobles works , make sure that this craft that you are pursuing leave behind a sort of a decent legacy for the upcoming generation that whom they will come after , make sure that the Goal that you are running behind are transcended and reach deeply in the heart the people who need to be inspire , never feel down to upgrade you goal or feel enough to reduce your plan size , writer down your Mastery plan Dream big and work with persistency and efficiency , work smart not hard this are the kind of aspect for any successful mind-set that you might need in your life .

Some said once a truly nice words about perusing Goals and Dreams and to this moment this word shake me from the inside of my heart and all around my body and I started to share this words with everyone I meet this words he said whereas follow :

((IF YOU KNOW THAT YOU WOULD NEVER FAIL HOW BIG YOU WOULD DREAM))

9- **never force anything** : it is Avery important flow of smartness in your life style and during your life , we face some time in our life when we feel that we urge some needs it could be love , materials or safety , we should never force yourself to get it , but rather we should tell our self that we are fully happy and good even if we could not reach to that needs , we can simply focus on the good side of our life , and shift our focus on positive and goods that we have owns rather than waste our time thinking about getting .

And here is the catch here

sometimes in our life

((we focus on what want and we neglect and forget to focus on what we really need , because what really serve us and makes us grow is close around us but we choose to focus on the things that make us temporally happy))

So if you just sit science for a small amount of time alone you start feel what you really want , only when you clear you mind and dive into your heart ,

If you wanted certain kind of thing in your life and for some reason it keep forced to out of our way then you have to realize that god is trying to insisted to you that this things is not what you really need .

10- **be authentic** : in your own world be who you are and don't copy any one around , do try to do something that you are everyone is trying to do but rather be the unique one who dream and has a vision to make

Try to be the blue shark in the ocean not the fishes in the sea, extract the love and talent that inside and feed it with love and hard determination , don't run behind materialistic and temporary items that can melt your true you and covers you with fake identikit and fake mask, break the rule and the commons tells and write you true life .

If you want to get a real life story you need why and when not how , you need the passion and strong desire and attract it , and only then you will build what you have meant you to be .

Give you self a break from all the things that you are suffering and stressing from , try to build a new way of thinking and views , precipitins of things , try to munificent the gym inside , and believe in yourself , because everyone to guide his self not everyone is guided .

((Not all wandering people are lost , not all lazy people are tired , and not all silence people are sad)) .

Life a is choices we choose the kind of dream we need we choose the people we accept to stay around with and we choose the place we go to , it every decision we make that makes the different in our mission to build our future in the right ahead days we always , our actions our habits and our relationship reflects our standard and our beliefs that hold inside and shape our reality .

Dare to dream and dare to smile and be happy in the middle of the storm.

Dare to help the one in need , dare to ask for assist in your life .

Make yourself aware of your actions .

Build your craft slowly and passionately .

Success in silence and celebrate outside .

Make your actions speak louder than your voices .

Live every day to the fullest never think of the day after it might not come s make this in your head as a reminder always .

Forgive when you can and focus on yourself not on the world .

www.ingramcontent.com/pod-product-compliance
Lightning Source LLC
Chambersburg PA
CBHW031317130726
47988CB00007B/2860